STEP UP TO RUN INCLUDES STORIES FROM:

Delaine Eastin

A professor, consultant, former Union City Councilmember, former California State Assemblymember, and the first Executive Director of the National Institute for School Leadership, Delaine Eastin was the first and only woman to date to be elected California State Superintendent of Public Instruction under Governors Pete Wilson and Gray Davis.

Myel Jenkins

Myel Jenkins is an engaged parent, community volunteer, and a professional with over twenty years of management experience in non-profit, foundation, and county government work. Jenkins has served in leadership position with the local high-school Parent, Teacher, Student Association, Black Women of Political Action, Sacramento, and the Women Democrats of Sacramento. She has also served her local school district as the Chair of the Curriculum and Standards Committee and as a Board Member of the San Juan Education Foundation.

Jackie Smith

With over thirty years business experience, Jackie Smith has served as a Commissioner and Legislative Representative on the Placer County Older Adult Advisory Commission and a Legislative Liaison for the California Alliance for Retired Americans. Smith also serves as a top-rated, sought-after realtor, serving predominantly seniors who are finding their forever homes with Realty One Group in Rocklin, California.

Tara Sreekrishnan

Tara Sreekrishnan is a nonprofit co-founder and brings professional public policy and community outreach experience at the city, county, and state government levels, with a focus on education, sustainability, and equity.

Dionne Ybarra

Dionne Ybarra is the founder of The Wahine Project, a nonprofit that has served over 6,000 girls and women since its inception in 2010 and brought a diversity of girls into a relationship with the ocean and with one another. Ybarra is the Chairperson of two appointed seats in Monterey County: The Commission on the Status of Women and the Civil Rights Commission

STEP UP TO RUN

WOMEN SHAPING THE FUTURE OF POLITICS AND PUBLIC POLICY

Pact Press

Published by Pact Press
Regal House Publishing, LLC
Raleigh, NC 27605
All rights reserved

ISBN -13 (paperback): 9781646032952
ISBN -13 (epub): 9781646032969
Library of Congress Control Number: 2021952117

Interior and cover design by Lafayette & Greene
Cover images © by C.B. Royal

Regal House Publishing, LLC
https://regalhousepublishing.com

Printed in the United States of America

Respectfully dedicated to all of the mothers, sisters, and daughters who step up to run

FOREWORD

By Lieutenant Governor Eleni Kounalakis

"You should run for office!" was a statement I heard many times as a successful young businesswoman from Sacramento. It was always flattering, and, truthfully, I even considered it. I had a passion for public policy, a track record as an activist, and a heart for service.

In 2009, I accepted an appointed position in the Obama administration rather than run for office myself. It was a conscious decision to get a job in public service rather than run. What held me back was very simple: Somewhere deep down, I was afraid that if I ran, I might lose.

Serving as a United States ambassador was the honor and privilege of my life and I thought I was headed for another chapter of service in what I—like so many others—was sure would be the Hillary Clinton administration.

But then, the unthinkable happened. The rise of bigotry and misogyny across the nation propelled Trump into office.

As a result, across the country, women stood up after the 2016 election and marched. The Women's March was the single largest one-day demonstration in the history of the world. The inspiration of that day led to thousands of women, like me, standing up, stepping forward, and running for office.

I often say that my decision to run was the least thought-through decision I've ever made in my life. Fear of losing completely melted away. I ran, and won—thanks to so many women, including the support of Senator Kamala Harris, Speaker Nancy Pelosi, and, yes, Secretary Hillary Clinton. With the help of these women, I became the first woman ever elected lieutenant governor of California, and together we brought down a high, hard glass ceiling. One year into the job, I could not be more honored to serve all the people of our beautiful state.

But as 2016 fades into the distance and 2018 was defined in history as "The Year of the Woman"—with the implication being it was unique and is now over—we must find new ways to inspire women and help them find the courage to run for office.

The stories in this book are critical for women around the country to read. They are stories of success—if not victory. The journeys of these five women are full of courage and conviction. They raised issues important for women and our families and pushed their opponents to match them on their commitments to progressive public policies. (I witnessed Delaine Eastin's remarkable campaign, as we frequently encountered each other in the most remote, rural parts of the state!).

In 2018, California elected three women as statewide constitutional officers for the first time in history: Treasurer Fiona Ma, Controller Betty Yee, and me. We also elected the most women ever to the California state legislature.

It was a huge victory. But we haven't yet reached gender parity, and we still have never elected a woman as governor in our state. The only way we reach gender parity is if women win. And the only way women win is if they run. So, to all the women out there who are looking for inspiration and the courage to run, you will find what you need in the stories of five amazing women.

THE LANDSCAPE OF WOMEN IN POLITICS

By Melanie Ramil

We used to talk about the numbers.

We would say: From school boards to the California State Legislature, women hold only 30 percent of all elected seats. In California, where we often pride ourselves on serving as the moral compass for the country, we have been led by zero women governors.

We used to talk about representation.

We would say: Women need a seat at the decision-making table because "if you're not at the table, you're on the menu." As women make up over half of the population, this needs to be reflected in who holds positions of power.

Yes, numbers matter. Yes, representation matters. But now, in the midst of a global pandemic, economic depression, and racial justice uprising, we finally give voice to the truth behind the numbers and beyond representation.

Women leaders are different. Women leaders possess a leadership style that is unique amidst the status quo. Women leaders are collaborative and effective and, simply, get things done.

Research has consistently found that women tend to adopt a more transformational leadership style, which is rooted in authenticity, cooperation, and a focus on the common good. As men have been at the helm of power since our nation's founding, we have only seen and thus have accepted as the norm a transactional leadership style, one that values self-interest over community and directive management over teamwork.

This is changing.

Over the last four years, to say there has been a shift in the undercurrent of politics in who we want and who we need to see in elected positions of power is an understatement.

When Hillary Clinton lost (the electoral college) in 2016 and Donald J. Trump was elected, the collective outrage that a man, who stoked fear through lies and racial slurs, admitted to sexual assault, and deepened divisions as a means to the most sacred office in our nation, propelled women into action. The marches that following January turned into a movement that manifested as political action committees raising funds to support women candidates, candidate training programs specifically designed for women, and organizations that set out to recruit and develop women political leaders. Women understood that the man in the Oval Office did not represent the heart and spirit of our nation, and we set out to change the narrative of who should be in office—not to ask for a seat at the table, but to demand and fight for the seats that are rightfully ours.

The ecosystem that began to build after the 2016 election proved its power on Election Night in 2018. From races for Congressional seats to statehouses to city councils across the country, women stepped forward as candidates like no other time in United States history. Two hundred and fifty-five women ran for House and Senate seats, and a record-breaking 117 women won. These victories resulted in a 116th Congress where women make up nearly a quarter of the elected body, the highest percentage in history.

The year 2018 was quickly deemed the second "Year of the Woman" following the strides made in 1992 when fifty-four women were elected to Congress—at that time, a figure that shattered records.

Across the country, we witnessed the highest number of women gubernatorial candidates in history. Of the nine women who currently serve as governor, five of them won in 2018, including Maine Governor Janet Mills and South Dakota Governor Kristi Noem, both were their state's first woman governor.

These themes saw parallels in every state across the nation, as thousands of women ran for local office—from school board to city council to county board seats. In California, Lieutenant Governor Eleni Kounalakis became the first woman elected to the post and eight women won seats in the state legislature, the biggest single leap for women in state history. Women now make up nearly 30 percent of the California State Legislature, the highest representation of women ever.

Alumnae of Emerge California, an organization that recruits and trains Democratic women, also made history. Of its 600 alumnae, ninety-two ran for office and fifty-six of them won, including Assemblymember Rebecca Bauer-Kahan—the first alumnae to win a seat in the California State Legislature.

In short, the status quo that led us to a Donald J. Trump presidency began to crack. And when you begin to shatter the status quo, and the beautiful tapestry that was caged within begins to reveal itself, you begin to celebrate a lot of overdue "firsts."

The thousands of women candidates that stepped forward to fight for our rightful place in the halls of power were all women who embodied the diversity of the nation. These candidates were Black women, Indigenous women, Brown women, transgender women, Muslim women, and millennial women. They were moms, grandmothers, attorneys, veterans, bartenders, and doctors. They were from big cities, suburbia, and the rural countryside.

Of the 117 women who were elected to Congress, forty-two identified as women of color, three identified as LGBTQ+, and a twenty-nine-year-old Alexandria Ocasio-Cortez became the youngest woman ever elected to Congress. Ilhan Omar and Rashida Tlaib became the first Muslim women elected to Congress, and Deb Haaland and Sharice Davids became the first Native American women elected to Congress. Ayanna Pressley became the first Black Congresswoman from Massachusettes, and Danica Roem became the first openly transgender person to serve in any U.S. state legislature.

Representation matters not for representation's sake. It is not to claim percentages, figures, or firsts. The firsts are not a victory unto themselves, rather they are a product of a paradigm shift and a message from the electorate. Rather, the firsts begin to allow the lived experiences of all people—Muslim Americans, millennials, moms, and Mexican Americans—to shape, bend, and upend longstanding policies that did not serve them in the past.

The years after the 2018 election brought us a global pandemic that shined a light on the disparities these extremist policies created and the economic depression that affected certain communities much harder than others. And we witnessed the "Great Reckoning," a national uprising that continues to demand an overhaul of the institutions that have created and perpetuated inequities in every single system upon which we build our lives—education, healthcare, criminal justice, housing, employment, and the list goes on.

These crises have removed the blinders and have exposed the leadership we have at the helm today. One only needs to take a glimpse at women leaders globally and locally to see that they are the ones truly leading through crisis. Their leadership is based on truth, compassion, integrity, facts, and science, on the desire to protect and serve the most vulnerable among them, and on the need to prioritize what is right and moral above their desire for re-election.

The outcomes show that when you elect women, you are electing leaders who are bringing their lived experiences to the dais with them as they vote, as well as a value set that prioritizes collaboration, innovation, community, and the common good.

If we want to live in a world that gives everyone the opportunity to succeed and recognizes the humanity of each and every one of us, we must elect women.

There is no doubt that the forces of the status quo, history, and the patriarchy in which we live today makes running for office as a woman a markedly different experience than that of men. Even though women candidates win at the same rate as men, they are left out of conversations when the establishment begins to search for a successor. When women do run, they then work exponentially harder in the face of sexism, misogyny, and the microaggressions that exist when one is actively working to shift the balance of power.

What does this mean?

As Congresswoman Ocasio-Cortez remarks in the documentary *Knock Down the House*, "For one of us to make it through, one hundred of us have to try."

The women in this book tell an important story that is often overshadowed by the celebration of the "firsts," the broken records, and the women political icons of 2018 we have come to love.

These stories represent the "99" who did not win on election night.

These stories represent how they moved the conversation forward and changed the narrative of the policy debates during the campaign, of how they forced the eventual winner to act on issues that would not have otherwise been discussed, of how their transformational leadership resulted in campaigns that valued young voices and uplifted fellow women of color.

The stories of the women in this book are not of an election victory, but rather—and arguably, more importantly—a cultural and moral victory that has ignited a movement. A movement that will inspire more women to see themselves as leaders, and to run, win, and lead in elected positions of power across the nation. It is only then that we will see an elected body that leads with grit, honesty, grace, and integrity, and one that will have the courage and fierce commitment to move us toward a more compassionate, just, and equitable world.

CANDIDATE DELAINE EASTIN

Office Sought: Governor
District/Municipality: State of California
Population: 38 million
Platform: Education, Environment, Housing, Transportation, Preschool-for-all, Healthcare-for-all, Free-College Tuition
Incumbent: None
Additional Candidates: Many other candidates ran, with at least two Republicans and eight Democrats
Personal Information: Age seventy, Caucasian

CALIFORNIA'S POLITICAL LANDSCAPE

Running for Governor in the largest state in the union is serious work. With more than thirty-eight million people in fifty-eight counties, I knew it was a heavy lift, especially for a woman.

Although California elects eight constitutional officers every four years, in 1994 when I was elected Superintendent of Public Instruction, only three women in total had been elected to a constitutional office in California since women got the right to vote in 1911. None had been elected Governor.

IN THE BEGINNING

I have known some real heroes. Some were teachers, librarians, managers, aunts and uncles, but my parents were my biggest heroes. My dad, Hank, was a six-foot-two Kentucky hillbilly with a nineteen-inch neck who was accepted into college but did not go. The year was 1931 and his father went bankrupt when their house burned down. So, my dad joined the U.S. Navy and sent money home to support his family. He served our country for twenty-two years. Hank was an amazing human being who taught me some of life's most important lessons.

Dotty, my mom and a fourth generation San Franciscan, was more urbane than my dad. She was an ardent believer in women's equality. My mother was petite, stylish, and thin, and, above all, she was a feminist. She and my dad made quite the odd couple in appearance but were in sync with their progressive values.

I was born in San Diego, where my dad was stationed. An oft-repeated joke told by my dad was that the hospital in which I was born was not named until they had me. The doctor took one look at me and exclaimed, "Mercy!" which gave the hospital its namesake. We moved several times, finally to the San Francisco Bay Area, where my dad was stationed, and lived with my grandparents. My older brother and I attended San Francisco schools for two years. My dad got out of the Navy in 1955, when I was seven years old, and we moved to San Carlos, where the schools were better. I left a classroom of forty-four in San Francisco (where I was leading a reading group) to join a second-grade class of twenty; it took me the rest of the year to catch up to the rest of the class. That is why I fought for K-3 class sizes of twenty or less when I became Superintendent of California schools.

I was raised with a strong work ethic and a love for literature as well as a spirit of optimism that has always remained with me and allowed me to better overcome obstacles and challenges.

Despite the odds stacked against me—our blue-collar family had few resources—I attended and graduated from UC-Davis. And then I went on to graduate school at UC Santa Barbara—all because my parents dared to dream. Later, I set up scholarships at both schools: at Davis for a woman who is the first in her family to go to college, because I knew what that meant, and at Santa Barbara for a graduate student in the School of Education.

When I left for UC-Davis in 1965, I could not borrow money under the College Student Loan Act because the law stated that women could not borrow money until they were twenty-one, while men could borrow at eighteen. My parents had to borrow money at 7 percent interest to pay my tuition. If I had been a male student, I could have obtained a student loan at 4 percent per year, with ten years to pay it back. By the time

I was twenty-one and could borrow the money, my parents' student loan payment was twice their house payment.

In the 1970s, one of my first jobs out of graduate school was teaching part-time at a couple of community colleges: De Anza College in Cupertino and Canada College in Redwood City. I was driving 1,000 miles a week most weeks, trying to get a full-time teaching job. I had some terrific mentors, and they told me to start new initiatives at the colleges to increase visibility as well as my chances of getting a full-time position.

I became the Women's Studies Coordinator at one campus and the Women's Reentry Coordinator at another. I developed internship programs, developed classes on community organizing and women in politics, and successfully wrote grants.

When I was twenty-six, I got appointed to the Planning Commission in Union City, where my husband and I bought our first house. I enjoyed participating in the commission meetings, asking questions and making a difference.

A year or two later, the only woman on the city council asked me to be her campaign manager in her bid for re-election. I told her I did not know how to do that, and she said, "We will teach you everything you need to know." On the night she was re-elected, she said, "And in two years, we are running you!"

And so, I looked into running for city council. A little bit of research told me I needed a more stable work environment to successfully run for office. I would need to change employers. Though I had finally been selected for a full-time teaching position, the San Mateo Community College board froze all new hires after Proposition 13 passed, and that job went away. If you are going to run for city council, you need a stable day job, and my jobs as a part-time freeway flyer, teaching at different locations with unpredictable schedules, did not provide the environment I needed for a successful run. I went into the private sector with the encouragement of my mother-in-law who told me the company she worked at, a public utility, was looking to promote more women and minorities.

That new job gave me the financial resources that made

running for city council more feasible. I remained on the planning commission but started laying the groundwork for my race for a seat on the council. By the time the election came around, there were seven candidates for three seats, with three incumbent male candidates. Another candidate was a woman who had lived in town for more than twenty years and was head of the Union City Chamber of Commerce. Talk about a grassroots campaign—my friends and I knocked on doors and put up signs. When the dust settled, the top two vote getters were the other woman and me. That year, 1980, we were the only city in Alameda County with a female majority on the city council: Three of five council members were women. That also reinforced in me the belief that gender matters in elected office.

And the third seat? It was a dead tie between two incumbents. To resolve the tie, the winner was decided by a coin flip, just as the California State Constitution called for. So the next time someone says their vote doesn't count, please remind them that it does.

Serving on the city council was a wonderful experience. We forged a partnership between the city and the school district with the help of my neighbor, who was the chief of police.

As a result of this partnership, James Logan High experienced a great increase in attendance, resulting in more income for the school district. Graduation rates went up when attendance improved. College attendance rates also went up and daytime crime dropped 33 percent within the first year. Within five years, James Logan High was a top ten feeder high school for affirmative action at UC-Berkeley. We built schools on city park grounds and co-maintained them, saving both the school district and the city precious resources.

We were, at that time, the fastest growing community in Alameda County. Not all the council members wanted to represent the city on the many boards we belonged to, so I had the opportunity to join more boards than other members. Thus, I learned a great deal about solid waste, transportation, libraries, regional government, and more.

I had always been passionate about electing women, and I helped to found, and then chair, the National Women's Political Caucus (NWPC) chapter in Southern Alameda County. We started running more women for city council and school board. Later, I ran to be the chair of the 18th Assembly District Committee of the Democratic Party, and won.

In 1986, the year I ran for the state assembly, women had had the vote in California for seventy-five years, but there had only been a total of thirty-one women who had served in the state legislature, including the eleven that currently were in office at that time. No woman had been elected to the 18th Assembly District Committee in the state's history. Leona Egeland had represented part of Santa Clara County when she spoke to my community college class in the mid-1970s. When asked if there was a women's caucus in the legislature, as there was in Congress, she said, "Well, if we called ourselves a caucus, we could meet in a phone booth. We are both happy a third woman has joined the legislature." At that point there had never been a woman in the State Senate. In fact, they remodeled the Capital building at about that time and did not put in a women's bathroom.

In the 1986 election, four Democratic women were looking to run for a total of eighty Assembly seats across the state. Two were allowed to go before the Democratic caucus to ask for their endorsement while two were initially denied, mostly for being too liberal. I was one of those denied. Fortunately, four women, with whom I had worked, stepped up and demanded I be allowed to make my case to the Democratic caucus because of my work within the party and the NWPC. Against all odds, I won the endorsement and the Assembly race.

That year included the biggest class of women in the history of the California State Legislature. With the addition of five of us, three Republicans and two Democrats, the total number of women rose from eleven to sixteen, the highest in our state's history, and we were featured on the cover of the California Journal with the title "A Capital Class."

While in the legislature, I chaired the Legislative Women's

Caucus and we discovered we got a great deal done across the aisle. I also chaired California Women Lead—then called California Women for Elected and Appointed Office—and we dramatically increased membership by reaching out to women on school boards, who had been largely overlooked in recruitment.

Later, in 1994, I became the fourth female to be elected as a statewide constitutional officer in California history, serving as State Superintendent of Public Instruction. It was also the first time two women were elected at the same time as constitutional officers in the state's history; the other became our State Controller. As of 2019, I am thrilled that three of our eight constitutional officers are women, for the first time in history. As a lifelong champion of electing women to public office, this is cause for celebration.

My first run for Superintendent of Public Instruction was no walk in the park. At that time, then Governor Pete Wilson went after immigrants through Proposition 187, which would have turned teachers into immigration agents. I opposed Prop 187. When it eventually passed, the night I was elected, Pete Wilson challenged me to enforce it. I said, "I will see you in court." Subsequently we won the lawsuit, but Democrats had lost the majority in the lower house and five of the eight constitutional officers were Republican. Governor Wilson may have won the electoral battle but he lost the political war; droves of Latino residents became more motivated than ever to participate politically, many, over time, re-registering from the Republican Party to the Democratic Party.

Still, we pressed on and won some tense battles. I challenged Pete Wilson on two other anti-immigrant initiatives: Prop 209 and Prop 227. The former ended affirmative action, and the latter was supposed to end bilingual education. While they both won a majority vote, I was able to grant all dual language immersion schools a waiver to offer second language instruction for those in bilingual schools. Thankfully, if all parents favor a pedagogic approach, the Superintendent of Public Instruction can grant a waiver. I am happy to report that in 2016, the voters overwhelmingly reversed Prop 227.

In the short run, Governor Wilson and his anti-immigration allies succeeded in turning California into a red state but, in the long run, he actually helped to turn California bright blue.

The election in 1998 was my toughest election in many ways. Although I had accomplished many things in my first term—K-3 class size reduction; the first ever statewide standards in English, math, science, and history; reinstatement of statewide assessments; task force recommendations for universal preschool; planting gardens in over 3,000 schools and improved nutrition—it was a time of significant personal upheaval for me. I was devastated by the end of my marriage to my husband of thirty years, and by the end of 1998, I found myself off-balance.

In the final two weeks of my 1998 re-election campaign, six wealthy men poured a million dollars into a campaign sneak attack against me, supporting a woman who one of the state's leading newspapers described as "not remotely qualified." Just when we thought we were done fundraising, we had to ramp up big and fast. With laser focus, we won that day and managed to carry the flag for children for four more years. After that, although I felt there was still a great deal to be done in California, I could not fathom running again without my husband at my side, so I left political life.

After my term was up, I became the first executive director of the National Institute for School Leadership in Washington, DC. After the successful launch, I came back to California as a Distinguished Visiting Professor of Educational Leadership at Mills College and an advisor to Mills President Janet Holmgren. Later, I stepped down from Mills to support two elderly aunts and to do some speaking and consulting. I did not picture another political run in my future, although I remained politically active. I served on the Rutgers Project 2012 to elect more women nationwide after reapportionment. I spoke at Emerge, Ignite, and the NWPC statewide conference. Then I chaired Close the Gap, to elect more Democratic women in California. We added a Democrat but lost seven Republican women, so our representation was still below 30 percent; America was below many other first-world countries.

Before I ran for governor, I had run fourteen campaigns and won fourteen times, including winning twice the seat of Superintendent of Public Instruction, the first, and still the only, woman to hold that job. However, when I decided to run in 2017, I had been out of politics for more than a dozen years and was not exactly a household name. Still, I decided to run for children and families, for our seniors and our homeless, for the environment and for infrastructure reinvestment. I knew it would be almost impossible to pull off a victory, but I ran because I am an optimist and I believed I could change the conversation and insert my vision for our great state.

WHY I RAN

When I was a kid growing up in San Carlos, California, with a father, who was a union machinist and a mother who worked as a dress clerk, we definitely weren't rich, but we also weren't poor. I became the first person in my direct line to graduate college, and I managed to do it with little debt, in part because of my parents' generosity.

During that time our state had a budget that reflected our democratic values. We invested in our children, and we invested in our roads and bridges and mass transit systems. Housing was affordable and accessible, healthcare was mostly paid for by generous benefit plans, our mentally ill were protected from homelessness, and our prisons were but a small line item.

We took care of our children, our communities, and each other in order to build a better tomorrow, and we fought for civil rights, women's rights, and (admittedly much later) the rights of our LGBTQ brothers and sisters. That's what being a Democrat means to me.

When I ran for my first statewide election in 1994, you want to know how much I raised? $3,000,000—not a paltry sum, but not exactly close to the $100-plus million Meg Whitman spent when she ran for governor in 2010. It did not manage to buy her the governor's mansion. How much does it cost our democracy when politicians are forced to ask people for obscene amounts of money to run their campaigns?

If politicians are spending all their time fundraising and mingling with the folks capable of writing these checks, you know where they aren't going? They aren't going into their communities. They aren't going to meet the people actually living in this state.

If they did, I can tell you they'd learn a lot. I know I did back when I visited all fifty-eight counties during my tenure as Superintendent of Public Instruction. And I've continued to learn ever since.

Education is the single most important investment California should be making, and I ran because I was appalled by not only how far America had fallen behind the rest of the First World, but how California, specifically, had stepped away from its historic commitment. I ran because none of the male candidates paid much more than mild lip service to our children and their education.

I ran for governor because I want every child in California to have the opportunities I had—to learn, to be mentored, to be inspired. When what is best for the children is at the center of every decision—whether in social services, education, the environment—we get the best for our entire beautiful state. This is something I have lived and something I know in my core. I wanted to change the discussion on the California political stage, and maybe even break the glass ceiling to become the first female governor, as I had done when I became the first female State Superintendent of Public Instruction, and only the fourth female constitutional officer in our state's history. I feel so fortunate to have had that opportunity to be heard and to influence the discussion.

I ran for governor in 2018 because I am an optimist, and I did not see anyone in that big field of candidates talking about education in the state of California. It was the elephant in the room—we had gone from our position at the top of all states in per-pupil spending to the near bottom. This, despite our celebrated generosity coming out of a Depression and a World War. Yet the candidates for governor, including the Democratic candidates, were ignoring education, which, I believe, has always been a key ingredient for California's future (and past) success.

When I moved to my second-grade class at Brittan Acres Elementary School in the 1950s, there was a nurse at the school who called my mother and told her to have my eyes examined. My mother did, and because of the school nurse, I got glasses. I walked out of the ophthalmologist's office and was surprised to see the leaves on the trees from so far away.

The librarian at Brittan Acres was Miss Firth. She said to me one day, "Honey, you seem to like to read, may I recommend some books for you?" I said yes, and she directed me to reading biographies, especially about successful women.

When I got to Carlmont High School, I was called into the counselor's office the first day of ninth grade. The counselor, Mrs. Chapman, asked why I was not in University Prep. I explained I was in College Prep because I wanted to go to college. She said that was not good enough to get into many higher education institutions that I might qualify for. Because of Mrs. Chapman, I changed to University Prep classes and went on to graduate from UC-Davis. My parents were not college educated, and they could not have given me the guidance Mrs. Chapman offered. To this day, I am thankful that she was there for me.

Today in California, our class sizes are among the largest in the nation and the ratio of nurses, counselors, and librarians to students trails the nation. The nurse, the librarian, and the counselor who changed the course of my life are no longer in many schools. While other states and other countries are busily improving their education systems, California has been disinvesting and losing its way.

As I have said for four decades, budgets are statements of

values, and I know that statement resonates with thoughtful people across California. It is disgraceful to be near the bottom in per-pupil expenditure but number one in per-prisoner expenditure.

We saw the campaign conversation change when I entered the race; education was finally given its due. In addition, my progressive stances on homelessness, child development, healthcare, the environment, and other issues were heard on the debate stage, and moved the needle on those issues in a more progressive direction.

At least part of the problem in politics is that too many people don't know the difference between expense and investment. Look at the budget of our state the same way you look at your family budget. Of course, we should hold expenses down, but we have to know when to invest. And we have got to work on substantive debates between candidates for these important roles. The ability to communicate the ideas of a candidate should not be a contest about who can raise the most money. To put it simply, we need campaign finance reform—a concept I have been fighting for my entire career.

Our strategy for a brilliant future for the next generation, and the next and the next after that, means we need long-range planning and sensible public policy.

That means our first budgetary priority as a state should be education. For those who have taken the time to read the state constitution, they know that it says, "From all state revenues there shall first be set apart the moneys to be applied by the State for support of the public school system and public institutions of higher education" (Article XVI, Section 8-California State Constitution). Too many people who take the oath to uphold and defend that document have not read it.

So, what did I learn from this campaign for governor? Like most large states, California has never had a woman governor. And, as a political science professor and a long-time advocate for electing women, I knew it would be a heavy lift. What I did not expect is what a huge difference it would make to women—

and girls—to see a woman on the stage in the debates. Holding her own and, according to what many people told me, winning those debates. We need to be in the room—it matters. I expect to see more women running next time, just as we are seeing more women entering the presidential race. Stepping up matters, and I am so glad that I did.

I had been off the stage for a long while. If I had been a person with individual wealth, I might have been able to buy more airtime, but lacking an official title after fifteen years away from political office was problematic unless I had the resources personally to get more airtime. Money matters. And I will keep pushing the message as I have for decades that we need campaign finance reform.

Fundraising was a challenge. The maximum contribution a single candidate for governor may receive is $29,200. And that's just for the primary. There are very, very few people able to raise that much money. High-level fundraisers were hesitant to step up to join my campaign—some because they had clients in other races who were connected to the managers of some of the other gubernatorial campaigns, some because they did not see a path to the top two in the primary. At the end of the day, our fundraising was not at the level required to win a statewide race in California.

In addition, while no one had more capable and enthusiastic supporters than me, we did not have the resources to "staff up" to the level needed for a statewide campaign.

Third, there was still a lot of the "Old Boy's Club" in evidence, leading to many frustrating moments. I received a call from a member of one of the labor councils who raved about my endorsement interview, saying it was the best he had seen in over two decades. When I asked why they hadn't endorsed me if that were the case, he said they did not see my path to victory. I noted that with that endorsement, I might have had a path to victory. Time and again, I heard a variation on that theme, from newspapers and from various organizations and membership groups. Even from old friends. If I had been a man, I and others believe I would have been received differently. Many around me believed that we were making a difference; during debates the other candidates so often said things like, "I want to second what Delaine said..." or "As Delaine just stated, I think we need..." or "I want to echo Delaine's comment." My campaign manager even created a great advertisement about it. Sadly, we lacked the resources to show that ad very many times.

So, in summary, I lost the race for governor because I had been off the scene for too long and I did not have the resources to have the breadth and depth of campaign infrastructure to win the most populous and most expensive state race in the nation. I am still so glad that I ran.

I do take great comfort in knowing that we changed the conversation in the campaign. I also take great pride in the amazing people who believed in our campaign and who gave their whole hearts to the race. I met retired teachers and seniors as well as first-time citizen voters and young women and men who were on fire to change our world for the better. I met people who have since run for office and who are ramped up to improve and enhance California.

I am forever grateful to those dreamers and doers who helped to inspire their fellow citizens to ask what they could do to improve our communities and our neighborhoods, our schools and our state.

It is time for Californians to start dreaming again. Let us put the gold back into the Golden State, sooner rather than later, with common sense investments in education, child development, housing, transportation, the environment, and healthcare for all.

Whether you are a first generation Californian or a fifth generation Californian, we owe it to the next generations of California to have the same amazing opportunities that so many of us had because people dared to dream.

ON THE CAMPAIGN TRAIL

I enjoyed the campaign trail. I found I usually traveled with upbeat people who believed in our mission. There were stressful moments but being surrounded by positive people on a mission makes for a wonderful experience.

I was fortunate in my campaign staff, despite some fundraising shortcomings.

We moved around the state enthusiastically, and I am proud to say we received the endorsement of a majority of the local Democratic clubs we appeared before.

The debates were perhaps the most frustrating, as time and time again, people in attendance proclaimed me the winner, often hands down. But that night on the evening news, I was often given short shrift and sometimes was not mentioned at all. Time and again, my debate contenders would second what I was saying or repeat what I said.

One of the most inspiring parts of the campaign was having teachers and students, school administrators and parents, former staff and long-time friends, people I did not know and people who I knew only briefly, stand in line to thank me for something I had done in the past or for running in this gubernatorial race because of my emphasis on education and children, families and healthcare, the environment and infrastructure. I felt so uplifted by those who came up to me to thank me. I am forever grateful to those who opened their homes, their backyards, and their wallets. I know of no campaign that had more heart. In the end, while we did not make it into the top two, the campaign trail was a glorious avenue to travel on.

MEMORABLE MOMENTS

In the first major debate, we were in San Diego appearing before the California School Board Association (CSBA). There were thousands of people in the room. We had been asked to arrive forty-five minutes early. Everyone was there on time except one of the candidates. He showed up after we were already on stage. He walked past my outstretched hand and walked over to another prominent candidate to shake his hand. He ignored all the other candidates as if signaling, this is between him and me.

At one point we were asked if testing had an important role to play and what that role should be. That same candidate who had ignored my outstretched hand stepped up and called for more testing and a system for holding teachers' noses to the grindstone if the results were not good enough. He said we should fire the bad teachers and give bonuses to the good ones, but that testing should be dramatically increased.

I was the next to speak. I said, "My dad always taught me you don't fatten a hog by weighing it more often." The laughter in the room was infectious. I went on to point out that the candidate was perhaps unaware that, if anything, we have a teacher shortage and to do wholesale dismissals would hardly improve education. We needed to make certain that teachers, while held to genuine standards, are in classes with fewer students, and in schools with more nurses, counselors, and librarians. Yes, we needed standards in English, math, science, and social science, but we also needed them in the arts. I went on to say that in the future more than 25 percent of the jobs in the new economy would be arts-based and so we needed to provide our students opportunities in the arts, drama, civic engagement, and athletics. The CSBA attendees were encouraging.

Because I had entered the governor's race with education as my centerpiece, one of my favorite moments was in Los Angeles, a month or so before the election. The candidates had been invited by the African American Methodist Episcopalian (AME) organization to engage in a forum. At one point, Antonio Villaragoisa gave me a great shout-out, thanking me for expanding the campaign's conversation to include education, adding that because of my advocacy, he had taken the time to look at the research and he was committed to expanding preschool and child development. I was most gratified and felt proud that I had moved the needle on education policy during the campaign.

There were several other memorable moments. At a central labor council meeting I was feeling particularly on point and came away with real optimism, especially after the Service

Employees International Union (SEIU) representative said it was one of the best exchanges she had ever seen. She was sad to report that only SEIU voted to give me the endorsement, not the labor council, even though, behind closed doors, they all agreed I had been the best candidate. And so it went.

ELECTION DETOX

The election was held in June and I was not in the top two. This was not a surprise. I had been before labor unions and women's organizations and a host of different campaign gatherings and there was not the momentum that was needed to raise the money, buy the ads, or change the trajectory. I was frustrated, of course, and felt the lack of endorsement by both labor and the National Organization for Women (NOW) most acutely. NOW endorsed a notoriously sexist candidate who did not promote women.

But I was surrounded by dear friends and family, and I took joy and comfort from the loyalty of my friends from hither, thither, and yon. My oldest friend, Karen, came out from Texas and others came from around the state. To quote Yeats—"My glory was I had such friends."

My response to the loss was to pick myself up, dust myself off, and begin supporting candidates, especially women, in down-ticket ballots around the state. I supported high-profile California races, but I was particularly active in local and district races. I also spent some time and energy devoted to thanking friends and supporters who had gone the extra mile.

Right after the primary, Gavin Newsom, the winning Democrat, graciously asked me to have dinner with him and his wife. During dinner, we spent some time on the most important issue for California: education. But then I turned the conversation to the challenges of waking up some ossified agencies, e.g., DMV, CalTrans, and EDD. Within the next few months, DMV did, in fact, run up against some enormous challenges; my concerns were valid.

I took comfort that Newsom's first partner, Jennifer, was

engaged in the issues at hand. While I sincerely think it is time to see women in leadership positions across our state and our nation and around the world, I do find that men of quality are not threatened by women of equality, and I am enthused that Newsom's wife is indeed a partner to him and that many of his appointees are strong women.

I know, as you do if you are taking the time to read this book, how critical it is to have women's voices at the table. To quote a modern proverb, *If you are not at the table, you are probably on the menu.* I am well aware that having women as leaders in education, business, politics, nonprofits, healthcare, policing, and crime prevention makes a great difference.

I have clear memories of attending the University of California at Davis, where the only tenured female political science professor was the professor who urged me to go to graduate school. I was surprised when I got to graduate school at UC-Santa Barbara and there were only three women in the graduate class of 100 and no tenured female faculty at all. It was that UC-Davis professor who made the difference for me in pursuing that graduate degree. I have tried to be that voice of encouragement in every position I have held and in my role as a mentor, as I well understand how the many mentors who helped me throughout my life, including some fine men, made all the difference.

That is one of the reasons today's conversations about women leading is important. We need to give shout-outs to our female pioneers who are often invisible, not noticed, not acknowledged for their contributions. I am encouraged when I see more people making an effort to acknowledge women, and I look forward to the day when it is not the exception.

As Thomas Jefferson said, "Men of quality are not threatened by women's equality," and I have worked with many fine men throughout my career. We still need more women in decision-making positions in government, business, the military, nonprofits, and elsewhere because it is better for everyone. I know from feedback that it made a difference to women and girls that I was on that debate stage in the governor's race. I look forward to more women being there in the coming gubernatorial races and to having more women as governors, especially in larger states, where only three of the eleven largest have ever had a woman in that role.

We've come a long way, but there is still much farther for us to go. We know that many of our female professors start off in a hole, receiving much less funding for their labs and research projects than their male colleagues.

In order to tackle this and other issues around diversity in STEM careers, I recently served on UC-Davis Chancellor's Women in STEM Advisory Board, alongside the first female UC-Davis Chancellor. We worked to support female faculty as well as encourage women to consider careers in STEM. Our UC-Davis efforts paid dividends, as UC-Davis came in first in the nation on best value colleges for women in STEM.

I am encouraged that Governor Newsom has embraced policies that I have long advocated for, including paid parental leave, expanded (and, hopefully, universal) preschool, full day kindergarten, and moving juvenile justice under social services. So, I ask you, please, help us build political parties that uphold our values. Yes, let us be so sexist that we support equal opportunity for all. Yes, let us insist the Democratic and Republican Parties stand up for great preschool, K-12, higher education, and school-to-career opportunities for all. Yes, let us insist that we build more affordable housing for all. Yes, let us demand that every single Californian has clean air and water and is environmentally committed to future Californians. Healthcare should be a right not a privilege. And, yes, let us promise that all people of every age, race, and sexual orientation receive the promise of fairness and justice.

Never forget, we are Californians and we must stand up for what is right by standing up for progressive social values, equality, and justice. That is how we got here.

Rising from the Ashes

We saw some dramatic changes in the years leading up to the 2018 governor's race, but we've still, at the time of this book's publication, seen only one woman make it into the runoff for governor and she was defeated.

When the dust settled from my race for governor in the primary in California, thirty-two candidates were on the ballot. California's top two primary candidates (only the top two candidates go on to the general election) resulted in Gavin Newsom and John Cox going on to November. Newsom, a Democrat, was victorious with 61.95 percent of the vote and Cox, a Republican, came in second with 38.05 percent of the vote. More than twelve million votes were cast. And the race was won by the largest margin since Earl Warren was elected in 1950.

The race was always a long shot for me. I had been out of politics for fifteen years and was not in a visible position in the state. Many people did not know who I was. I ran knowing what a stretch it was because, when I entered the race, the other candidates were all male and were not discussing what I considered one of our most important missions as a state: to care for and educate our children.

I believe I started too late and without enough underpinnings. Again, I am not sorry I ran because I believe I fundamentally influenced the policy conversation and improved the trajectory of public policy in California, especially as it relates to our children. I met amazing people and had incredible experiences. I have no regrets. This new administration with its stance on parental leave, focus on early intervention, full day kindergarten, and its action to move juvenile incarceration to social services, as a few examples, gives me hope.

Gavin did change the trajectory of his remarks, and I am grateful that he has kept his word on increased preschool investment. His increased investment in K-12 and higher education is heartwarming to say the least, but it is not enough. We must elect more members to the legislature to fight for education as well as for affordable housing, healthcare for all, our precious environment, and to push for infrastructure modernization.

The bottom line: elections must change from electing the best candidates that money can buy to just electing the best candidates. The dangers of money and influence determining outcomes are not just apparent in California and America but in too many places and in too many circumstances. Let us rationally build a system of debate and discussion where outcomes are decided by intelligent discussions instead of the best government money can buy.

CANDIDATE DIONNE YBARRA

Office Sought: Mayor
District/Municipality: City of Pacific Grove
Population: 15,041 with many retired residents
Platform: Environment Leadership, Affordable Housing, Diversity, and Transparency
Opponents: Two incumbents, who were both retired white males and had each served one term. Both moved to Pacific Grove after retirement.
Personal Info: Mexican American, forty-seven years old, non-profit founder, appointed chairperson on County Commission, and a twenty-four-year Pacific Grove resident who has been a political activist for her entire adult life.

PACIFIC GROVE'S POLITICAL LANDSCAPE

Pacific Grove is a Monterey Peninsula City that is tucked in between better-known tourist destination towns, Monterey and Pebble Beach. It is a predominantly white, retired community recognized for its lack of diversity. A majority of the town identify as Democrats. I knew voter turnout would be down because it was not a presidential election. In the end, the retired white vote showed up at the polls.

As a new candidate it was important for me to consider when to announce my intention to run. Timing varies from city to city. In the town that borders mine, new candidates had announced months before I had even decided that I would run. This neighboring city is twice the size. Pacific Grove has more of a village feel and, historically, candidates announce themselves at the beginning of the summer prior to the November election. In 2018 the lack of affordable housing and the influx of short-term rentals were heavy on the minds of Pagrovians. Pacific Grove was due to begin considering its responsibility to our regional neighbors: how our decision-making not only affected the Monterey Peninsula but the entirety of Monterey County because of our location on the southern tip of the Monterey Bay. If we were to begin to consider big infrastructure changes that would bring in more residents and tourists, we would rely on the resources of the highways and cities, as well as the water system of all of the small and large cities that are the gateway to Pacific Grove.

As a lifetime resident of Monterey County, my work as a regional parent educator and my roles on boards (and most recently working in operations overseeing global work in Indigenous communities) over the last twenty years made me a capable candidate who would take into consideration our small-town contributions and responsibility to the greater good. I have lived in Pacific Grove as a renter, and a woman of color raising children, my entire adult life. Having fought for the rights of my community long enough to gain a national reputation, I felt it was time to expand the electoral ballot to include more diverse candidates. Although a retiree from the Chevron corporation eventually won the election, my candidacy brought environmental protection as a guiding principle to the forefront of discussion.

Even though I did not win, the process of running for electoral office has since galvanized my county-wide work to create positive change and enhance the wellbeing of my community.

IN THE BEGINNING

I came to the city of Pacific Grove in 1994. I was the twenty-four-year-old mother of a newborn and a four-year-old. My husband at the time was fresh out of graduate school and starting his career as a social worker. When we first rented an apartment in Pacific Grove, having moved from my hometown of Salinas, I felt some culture shock. I am Mexican American and had been used to the familiarity of being around my culture. Nothing in this new community felt relatable. But there were a lot of people our age and we had a close network of friends who had all grown up in the area and life became about making new friends. My new neighbor in the apartments next to me was a Muslim from Algeria—a student at an international college who was also married with a child. Each of us a fish out of water in our own way, we became supportive friends. Eventually, Pacific Grove enchanted me, with its narrow streets lined by historic beach cottages.

As a growing family we lived in a community, we created community, and we supported one another. Our town was truly "our town," as tourists turned around at the Monterey Bay Aquarium just north of us and headed back to scenic Highway 1. We had a coffee shop where we would spend time, knowing one another's names. We grew up there through our twenties, thirties, and forties. We watched one another date, marry, have children, divorce. We were of all ages, from many different places, each with our own particular story to tell. It felt as though the bohemian lifestyle still existed in the 1990s and I was a part of it.

I eventually found myself a single mother with three children. Wanting my kids to remain in the same school district, I was desperate to stay in Pacific Grove. After my divorce, we moved many times, but I was always able to stay close enough so that my kids could walk to school, to the library, the grocery store, friends' houses, and sports practices. I had to navigate through the town with a new concern for finances which, I felt, created a gap between myself and other community members. There were times our refrigerator only had eggs, tortillas, and butter in it. Some afternoons, I relied upon food from the local Catholic church. At times, I couldn't afford gas, so my car just sat, parked. My kids were once benefactors of free Christmas gifts from the local Lions Club International. I always wondered how the club knew we were that much in need. Part of me felt embarrassed and the other part of me just felt so grateful. My friends and my children's friends were buying homes, while I still rented. But thankfully, there were affordable options. From 2000 to 2010, I was able to afford several short-term housing options that cost just under $1,400 a month.

In the early 2000s, our town began to change. Houses sold more quickly, many of which were remodeled to fetch an ever-higher price. Rentals were becoming scarce, and I felt home insecurity for the first time, worried that we could be the next family to become displaced by an owner wanting to sell. Despite the unsettled feeling this gave me, I held comfort in the fact that I had been part of the community for over ten years, familiar with the people on the streets, in the library, at the post office, and in restaurants that were now a part of the fabric of our small town.

There was only one Head Start preschool, one elementary school, and one high school in Pacific Grove, and all three of my sons attended them. I had gotten to know the school staff and relied on a few of them for many years to see my children through. Once, after I'd left for work, when my oldest son didn't show up for his high school art class, his teacher went to our house, got him out of bed, and took him to class. (This teacher only told me this story after my son graduated.)

These were the relationships I relied upon, and that other parents relied upon, to help educate and raise our kids. There wasn't so much trouble for our kids to get into that someone else didn't see and report back to their parents—not to get them in trouble but to keep them safe. To this day, my adult kids are friends with the youth they went to preschool with as well as their parents. We still run into one another at the meat counter at the local market or the farmer's market on Mondays. We update each other on what our kids are up to, and we reminisce a bit about the days we shared at Lover's Point, the quintessential family beach where our toddlers could run around naked while our preschoolers played in tide pools. How lucky were we and how privileged!

There is no doubt that I, as a Mexican American and second-generation daughter of a migrant field worker, had stumbled into white privilege. Someone in my town once referred to me as "not that kind of Mexican." They didn't know that I had been pulled over more times than I could count in my red beat-up hatchback, the bumper with its broken taillight attached by duct tape. I was on food stamps at the time and couldn't afford to fix a dent on my car. Once, I was pulled over en route to my son's friend's house—I had to tell him that his grandfather had passed away. After sitting in the car for twenty minutes, waiting for the officer to approach, and feeling increasingly anxious about the news I needed to share with my son, I got out of the car to ask what was taking so long. The police officer warned me that I would be tazed if I didn't get back in my car. I couldn't imagine this happening to a Caucasian woman in a different type of car. The police officer finally let me go without a citation, and I was never told why I had been pulled over in the first place.

A dear Nigerian friend once told me that he stopped coming into Pacific Grove because he would get pulled over every time he drove through. Just recently, one of my employees, who is Mexican American, shared that while walking with two friends, she was stopped by police officers who asked for her documentation. These issues of equity before the law in Pacific Grove are still relevant to this day. While I loved my town for its increasing diversity of new Asian and European residents—we were friends and neighbors with the families, students, and professors from the Defense Language Institute at Middlebury College, and international graduate students from The Naval Postgraduate School—I could and still do feel an undercurrent of racism and classism toward people of color that not even "America's Last Hometown" could escape. These issues motivated me to be a voice of color for our community. I believed being the city's mayor could bring systematic change to the institutions in the city that were allowing this racial disparity.

In 2010, the remodeled houses, selling for increasingly high prices, were pushing out single middle-class twenty- to thirty-year-old residents. The last of the young bohemians were gone, replaced by an influx of second-home buyers who wanted to retire in Pacific Grove, and who discovered the profits gained from the vacation rental market. Too many homes on the quaint little streets, ones that used to be occupied by single moms, dads, and the elderly, were now listed as vacation rentals.

With my sons grown and out of the house, I planned to travel and moved from Pacific Grove to the neighboring Peninsula City. I wanted to spend less on rent and Pacific Grove no longer seemed as appealing as it once had. I moved away for two years but, as fate would have it, I remarried and had another child at the age of forty-three. My in-laws were anxious to help us get back into Pacific Grove to take advantage of the highly rated school district. In just two years I had been entirely priced out of Pacific Grove, with rents that kept soaring. Between vacation rentals and military stipends that increased, landlords were finding they could get any asking price, especially when there was a statewide increase in the need for housing.

My husband and I realized we could no longer afford to rent. My husband's parents assisted us with a down payment so that our mortgage was affordable. This was the first time I was confronted by housing prices coupled with the responsibilities of home ownership. Now that we have lived in our home for almost four years, we know that we are very lucky that we were able to buy when we did; the prices just keep going up and up. Feeling so blessed to feel secure in our housing situation, I, once again, stumbled back into white privilege.

My deep desire to stand up for what I believe in and to want to help others is in my blood. My father was stationed in Vietnam when I was born, and he and I met just one time while he was on leave. He was killed by friendly fire in 1971 when I was three months old, just four months before he was due to end his time in the military.

The loss of my father left me broken in many ways. Who might I have been if he had lived? And I wonder if I am who I am because he died? For I have been molded and influenced by several individuals over the course of the last thirty years of my life—the first being my first-born. I was a single mother and twenty years old when my first son was born. I had received my father's GI Bill so I attended college at no cost, knowing that a college education would be my hand up in raising him.

The family I later married into also profoundly shaped my life. In my early twenties I was able to study at Esalen with my mother-in-law who led workshops. As her only daughter, she imparted to me the ideals of feminism, the teachings of Gloria Steinem, her experience fighting against the Vietnam War, and her time living in a commune. These fireside teachings, as I liked to call them, fueled my life and my passions.

When I was twenty-four, I heard a life-changing story on NPR about the rising movement of Latinos that was spreading across the country. I learned of a Latino Civil Rights March happening in Washington DC. My husband supported my desire to go, and so I did—with my toddler on my hip. When I returned, I became active with the local League of United American Citizens and attended local marches with my kids in tow, protesting on behalf of fieldworkers and unions. I believed that workers should have a quality of life that included safe working environments, fair housing, fair wages, and overall respect. I sought opportunities to work on local campaigns in opposition to Proposition 187, which prevented undocumented citizens from using public healthcare services except in an emergency, and Proposition 209, along with local candidates who I believed in. For the first time in my life I was shedding the shame that my family was Mexican American— shame that I was ashamed to feel. I was coming to understand the struggles my immigrant grandparents faced, the racism my family had experienced, as well as an ability to recognize the racism I encountered on a daily basis. My heart swelled while marching in Washington because I took on the collective pain and struggle of Latinos from every state in our nation. My life had a new purpose.

For nearly twenty years I had worked as a parent educator, believing that empowering parents would be my life's work. I supported women through childbirth as a birth doula and lactation educator. When I worked with women in hospitals, I was their advocate and I pushed for supportive legislation for women in their childbearing years. We worked on laws that supported breastfeeding in the workplace, doulas in hospital delivery rooms, homebirths, and vaginal births after cesarean deliveries in local hospitals.

In January of 2010, I began to advocate for girls and young women in a surprisingly new way: I started surfing.

After a lifetime of being terrified of the ocean—and watching my kids fearlessly surf—I took surfing lessons with a friend, which led us on an adventure to Mexico. We traveled to the state of Jalisco, not far from where my grandmother had been born, in the city of Guadalajara where she had been raised as an orphan in a convent. I appreciated my time there, knowing it was a privilege to return as a tourist after my grandparents had left the country to find a better life for their children. It has always weighed heavy on my heart that Mexico, a beautiful country to which I have now returned to countless times, was a place that my grandparents fled in order to find employment working in the fields. Become a fieldworker was a step up for them. This legacy will always remain humbling to me, and one that I hope my children will always hold within themselves.

Upon returning from this first trip, I had my "aha moment." In Mexico, I had overcome a paralyzing fear of the ocean, I'd met people from around the world, and I felt solidly connected to an appreciation for my past.

How in the world, I wondered, did a little brown girl from East Salinas find herself out on the ocean on a surfboard? How could I help other girls of similar backgrounds? How could I leverage what I perceived as being an imposter of white privilege? For one thing, I rarely saw girls on the water. My three sons were raised surfing with their dad, and I could count on one hand the number of girls I had ever seen riding the waves, and none were girls of color. In 2010, I founded The Wahine Project with a mission of eliminating the barriers that prevent a diversity of girls from a relationship with the ocean and with one another. In building foundational relationships in association with The Wahine Project, we have visited ten countries. Most of our outreach has taken place in California, predominantly focused in Monterey County. In the last five years, the term "surf equity" was coined, and I found myself being a voice for a movement and legislation that would bring equal pay to women in professional surfing. Within ten years, my organization has reached over 10,000 youth and women globally, with the effort focused on loving the sea so much that we will collectively take ownership in caring for it. This work led me to a position with The Nature Conservancy, the largest environmental nonprofit in the world, where I landed another dream job as an Operations Manager for an Indigenous Peoples and Local Communities Team. I was part of a global team that worked in twenty-two countries. The high-level environmental work that I was a part of took me to the jungles of Borneo where I was able to stay in a small village in the rainforest, witnessing firsthand the devastation of deforestation. Another trip took me to the Mayan forest in the Yucatan, where farmers were rebuilding after deforestation by working the ancient tradition of milpa to restore their land. All my work in the last ten years has been through global partnerships that are rooted in restorative justice.

WHY I RAN

When Hilary Clinton lost in 2016, I, like everyone else I knew, was devastated. I live in a very liberal Democratic community so our collective mood was defined by one overriding question: "What are we going to do now?"

I first ran for class representative as a freshman in high school. Two of us ran as a team. Being painfully shy, I relied on my teammate's outgoing personality to win the election. While I wanted to represent the student body, I didn't like attention. I credit our win to my ability to win people over, one small group at a time, and my teammate's ability to speak in front of larger crowds.

But when Donald Trump said, "Mexico isn't sending their best," I was driven to run for office. To this day, those words cut like a knife. Both sides of my family came to this country from Mexico, and two generations of my family members served in four wars. After one generation, we were graduating from college. After one generation, my grandparents were homeowners.

We are Americans, and we have always fought for the rights of anyone who needed a voice. I wanted to go big, and I believed that, with the right training and support, I could run. I asked lots of questions, sought the best mentors I could find, and put together a support team.

Midterm elections were fast approaching, and I learned that the incumbent mayor would not be running for re-election. There was already one woman on the City Council and three other women would also be running. The county of Monterey, however, had only ever had one female mayor. At that time, I was the Chair of the Commission on the Status of Women and the Chair of the Civil Rights Commission. Equity was the bottom line for me.

I decided to run for mayor, because this was the seat where we needed the voice of more women. My opponents would be two retired men who had been serving short terms on the city council. They had also lived in the city of Pacific Grove for only a short time. They were a member of the demographic of retired, professional white men. Both had retired and moved to Pacific Grove to live in homes they purchased, whereas I understood only too well what it took to try and stay in Pacific Grove as a single mother with three children. I had deep roots within the community. I knew more about my small town than the two of them put together.

I am also a staunch environmentalist, having worked in environmental protection for the last ten years. One of my opponents had just retired from Chevron while the other referred to me as an "ecologist" because he saw I carried a reusable mug. It was clear to me that neither of my opponents had any experience of environmental work.

My heart also ached for Pacific Grove's growing Latinx

population. Many local businesses depended on their work in the hospitality industry, but often our Latinx community did not feel they had been invited to the table. I wanted to offer them a seat.

I had worked on budgets for national and global programs and knew how those were managed. The executives of those organizations were held accountable with the highest level of transparency. Because of my experience, the oversight and accountability associated with the budget of a city of 15,000 people didn't feel daunting at all in comparison.

It was time to win over the hearts and minds of my community and to build a trust that couldn't be established, I felt, with the other candidates. I began to pursue partnerships with like-minded candidates from other peninsula cities; it was important to build these relationships from the get-go because if we all won we would be working together not only for our individual cities but for the well-being of our peninsula and our county. Our consensus would be imperative to our successes on our individual councils. How are our decisions here in Pacific Grove affecting our neighboring counties? To me, this collective agreement and consensus was the progressive thinking required by our city leaders.

ON THE CAMPAIGN TRAIL

My overall race was short in comparison to those women who had been working for months on their campaigns around the state of California. We began in mid-June, and I had a budget of $10,000, which I would need to raise. I had just completed an amazing training program for female Democratic candidates, and my first focus was to build my platform. A two-person team from Florida led me through a workshop that pulled together the pillars I would run on—transparency, community, and our environment. A committed group of six women met with me regularly to share how I could effectively reach their section of the community. We wrote, with the help of many others, over 5,000 postcards with personal messages to constituents. I was the only person running for mayor that regularly attended the farmer's market. I did this for six weeks, half of the campaign. It was nerve-racking, putting myself out there each week, but the relationship-building I was able to accomplish was phenomenal. I also created weekly coffee-shop talks and was available in ways that I intended to continue after I was elected.

I walked precincts and talked with the most wonderful people. Overall, I wish I had had more time for campaigning, but with a three-year-old child, I could only extend myself so much. My husband was very supportive and while he managed the home front, there were times when I had to cut precinct walking short to tend to the needs of my family. Family time is the first to get sacrificed on the campaign trail, and time away from my family was difficult for me.

MEMORABLE MOMENTS

For me, the highlights of my race occurred during the debates. I completed a two-hour interview with a panel from a popular weekly magazine, a group who are not known for pulling any punches. Two hours is a long time! I felt so strong and confident with my answers that, when I left the interview, I thought that if the campaign was to end at that very moment, I would be proud. The three of us running for office also assembled at a city candidate forum, where I faced both strangers and people who I had known in the community my entire adult life, in what was said to be the biggest showing of the community these forums had seen in twenty years.

One of my most humbling experiences was to receive the endorsement of our labor unions. This moment was also clouded with sadness as I wasn't able to share the news with my mother-in-law; she died several months before I announced my run. I had hoped she might be my co-pilot. After I received the endorsement, I immediately called her sister. It was a full-circle moment for me, having been made to feel as if I were one of their own, as if this family had passed me the torch that was lit from their lineage of female activists who risked their lives in the resistance in Russia. If this family could endure, and if my own grandmothers and great-grandmothers could risk their lives to bring their children to America in the 20s and 40s, then I could risk using my voice and not be afraid to be the most popular person in the room. I could question those in charge without fear of losing anything. I could stand in a room full of hundreds of strangers and tell them why I thought they should vote for me. If my own mother could dare to breathe again after she lost her husband in Vietnam, then I could do this. I had nothing to lose and everything to gain. I could do this.

The Election

I was supposed to be in Santa Fe, New Mexico, on election day for a three-day conference with my work at the Nature Conservancy. I was able to delay my trip by a day, but my flight was due to depart at six a.m. the day after the election.

I arrived early at the polls to put in my ballot, and the day moved past in a surreal way. I tried going to bed early, but I kept waking up every couple of hours to refresh the election results on my phone. By early morning, I knew I hadn't won. Initially, I felt sad, but because I had to prepare for a flight and my upcoming conference, I moved back into work mode. I was grateful to be surrounded by colleagues, who attended the conference from all over the world. It was a great distraction for me. For the next three days, when I was asked about the election, it was a quick, positive discussion, and we swiftly moved on to the work topics focused on what we can do to help save our planet.

Election Detox

When I returned home, I spent time with my husband to reflect on all that we had both experienced during the campaign. While we both talked of our disappointment at the outcome, we also expressed what made us grateful.

Rising from the Ashes

Beginning a year prior to the election, I served as an appointed commissioner on two Monterey County commissions. The seats I held were Chairperson for the Civil Rights Commission and Chairperson for the Status on the Commission of Women of Monterey County. In the city of Pacific Grove, I held a seat on our Recreation Commission—a seat for which was appointed by none other than the newly elected mayor who I had lost to in 2018.

In 2020 I was approached by a committee to run for City Council in Pacific Grove but decided to focus on the County of Monterey appointed seats I held, as well as stay focused on the growth of The Wahine Project. After talking it over with my husband, I initially thought to do it, but I changed my mind at the last minute when Covid hit the world and I needed to put my energy into saving my nonprofit. Like so many other nonprofits, we had to find a way to pivot the way we worked and served our community. June 2020 through August 2021, we adapted successfully and our program grew 200 percent, serving more families throughout Monterey County than we ever had in a one year time span. We also opened a store front and a community center to bring our work off the beach and into the community.

While not pursuing any elected position, my voice continues to challenge the status quo and the white patriarchy in my everyday work as a nonprofit founder. Every time someone advocates for diversity, we open doors for others. We keep standing on one another's shoulders, adding the strength of our voices to those who have gone before. We show others, so they can see what they can be.

CANDIDATE JACKIE SMITH

Office Sought: California State Assembly
District/Municipality: District 6
Population: 468,000
Incumbent: Thirty-four-year-old Caucasian attorney in his first term
Additional Candidates: None
Personal info: Sixty-three-year-old, LGBTQ+, realtor, notary, small-business owner; semi-retired, married to Darlene Smith, one son, Michael, age thirty-nine

CALIFORNIA DISTRICT'S POLITICAL LANDSCAPE

Assembly District 6 (AD6) is one of the most conservative of the eighty assembly districts of California. Placer (70%), El Dorado (12%) and parts of Sacramento (18%) counties combined represent over 468,000 residents. In El Dorado County alone the average age of a voter is seventy and they are predominantly Republican.

IN THE BEGINNING

Although my parents were Democrats, politics was never a big deal in our house. My dad was a milkman and a strong Teamster, but his loyalty to the party was all about the Union. Dad believed that it was important to stand up for workers. "Never cross a picket line or be a scab," he would say. "Buy union products whenever you can, and no matter what, always stay true to the Union."

In contrast, politics always intrigued me. As a youngster, I watched from the sidelines while my father yelled at the newscasters about politics and the war. "What the hell are they thinking?" was his usual refrain. Although usually a peaceful soul, he had his moments.

When I turned sixteen, in 1972, the Vietnam War was in full swing and long hair was the style of the day for my male friends, all of whom seemed to drive VW buses. I had waist-long hair and drove my parents' old white Plymouth Fury II to school. George McGovern, a Democrat, was running against Richard Nixon for president. Gas was forty cents a gallon and I remember my father always complaining that it was too high!

Much to my parents' dismay, I jumped right into politics.

For my history credit, I joined the team working on the McGovern campaign, and I've been hooked ever since. Stuffing envelopes, making calls on rotary phones, standing on street corners—it was exciting!

When McGovern lost, I felt the loss, but it was the energy of that campaign that sparked my interest in politics. That year at school, I received a community service award, and my call to service was born. I started a local division of the Sierra Club, was a Girl Scout leader, and even taught at the grammar school as a teacher's assistant, but for me nothing compared to the excitement of politics.

I attended college with aspirations to major in political science and become a lawyer. But my life took a different turn. I got married, started a family, had a son, bought a house. I finished my bachelor's degree in San Diego and worked as a full-time mom. I divorced my husband of twelve years and moved to the Silicon Valley where I worked in several industries in different capacities: advertising, semiconductors, and biotech.

But my interest in politics, and my determination to stand up for women's rights, never wavered. I contributed to the Democratic party in the Bay Area, attended rallies and functions. I never really dove back into politics, however, as I had done in my younger years. Then Hillary Clinton decided to run for president in 2008.

In 2008, I began donating regularly to Hillary Clinton's campaign after she announced her run for president. In fact, I went to her kickoff rally in Oakland to see her in person. It seemed surreal that a woman was running for president. The buzz surrounding her campaign was wild and I was thrilled. I felt in my heart that Hillary as our president would change everything. (That was the same year a young man named Barack Obama suddenly showed up in the political landscape and rapidly became a force to be reckoned with.)

In early January, I was working at a Fortune 500 biotech company in Santa Clara. I came home from work and turned on the news to a story about Hillary campaigning in New Hampshire. I couldn't believe what happened next. A man had disrupted one of Hillary's events, shouting and carrying a sign with the words IRON MY SHIRT! It was as if he'd personally designed his protest to turn me into an activist. How dare he say that to the most qualified and intelligent woman ever to run for office? I was livid.

I ended up traveling to five states to campaign for Hillary, spending thousands of dollars on hotels, flights, and meals. We fought hard on street corners, calling out to everyone who passed. It was a battle, but Obama won. When Hillary lost the Primary, I was devastated.

In 2008, I married my partner at the rotunda in San Francisco, worked in the Valley at the biotech company, and enjoyed the Obama years.

After working in biotech for twelve years, my company closed our division in Santa Clara. In the next few years, I graduated from UC-Santa Cruz with a business administration certification, lost my mom to ALS, and moved to Rocklin in Placer County in 2012 to start a career in real estate. But my political spark was rekindled in 2016 when Hillary decided to run again. And once again, I was all in.

I couldn't travel as I'd done in 2008, due to financial limitations, so I created a nationwide Hillary banner project; we had the same banner template and signs in fifty states. I was still able to attend the Democratic National Convention in Philadelphia, travel to four states, and direct endless rounds of canvassing and phone banking—whatever was needed to get the word out to help Hillary. My life was on hold to stand up for her to win. She was not only the most experienced candidate, but she was running against Donald Trump. Hillary was sure to win.

Or so we thought.

WHY I RAN

The months following November 2016 dragged. When Hillary lost to Donald Trump I felt like the country and I had been cheated. After all, she got three million more votes! We'd all worked so hard. It felt as though a death occurred, and I was left numb. The holidays were strange. Our whole world felt different somehow. We'd not yet begun to understand that our real political fight was only just beginning. I hadn't yet grasped the magnitude of the "fire of the fight" that Hillary had lit in my soul. Then came the Women's March of January 2017.

I decided to go Washington DC to protest Trump's inauguration and to attend the March. It was an experience I will never forget. That morning, before departing Washington, I visited JFK's eternal flame in Arlington in the pouring rain. *Ask not what your country can do for you, but what you can do for your country.* On the plane ride that day, I knew I had to get involved in politics in a more substantial way in order to effect positive change.

What could I do? I was a community organizer, businesswoman, real estate investor, a senior, a married LGBTQ woman. All I knew was that I was all in and ready to risk everything I had to fight for the disenfranchised, for our seniors, for the environment, and I vowed to stand up to hate every step of the way. I was ready to make my stand. I live in one of the most deeply conservative areas of California, so whatever I did, I knew I would have to be strong.

In the back of my mind, I kept asking myself, "What would Hillary do?" I decided to jump into local politics headfirst.

By the end of January 2017, the Placer County Democratic Party was selecting their delegate spots for the state party convention. Seven men and seven women were to be elected for a two-year commitment. I decided to run and this time—after giving my two-minute speech, and a vote in by a majority of voters at the caucus—I was elected. As a newly elected delegate, I was required to go to the state party convention and represent my district to vote on rules, bylaws, and policies. I joined the women's, senior, and LGBTQ caucuses. I was also elected to the LGBTQ Caucus Executive Board representing all LGBTQ Democrats in California.

Still not satisfied with my activism, I started the first ever LGBTQ Stonewall Democratic Club of Placer County. Our Placer Stonewall Democrats is an anomaly of sorts in this county, which is over 40 percent Republican, but as of this writing, we are still going strong with a large membership.

I've joined California Alliance for Retired Americans (CARA) and our California Dreamers, or DACA (Deferred Action for Childhood Arrivals) recipients. I marched in our March for Science, the Tax March, and Gay Pride parades in San Francisco and Sacramento. For every parade and march, I come prepared with felt fabric and a slogan for the day. My garage is now bursting with felt banners of varying colors and lengths, something for every occasion—still in the spirit of those early suffragists, even though the issues have expanded over time. I even published a book, *Tales from the Ironing Board: Hillary Clinton, the Inauguration and Me*, under a company I formed, Shattered Glass Press.

I began to look into exactly how you "run for elected office" and reached out to my mentors for advice. With their guidance, I've graduated from the EQCA Leadership Academy, taken Christine Pelosi's Campaign Bootcamp, and was part of the 2018 class of Emerge California, a women's group which recruits and supports female candidates. I was ready to serve in political office, but where and how?

After much research, I decided to run for the Sixth District State Assembly seat.

Our first-term incumbent representative was voting against practically everything that could help seniors, veterans, the environment, our housing burden, education, and healthcare. Our district—my district—deserved better. We needed someone who would vote for housing for our seniors and veterans, for drug transparency, and for healthcare for all. We needed someone who would stand up for diversity and inclusiveness, who believed that we can make a difference, even at the local level.

With my business and life experience, I knew that I was the right voice for those issues, and it seemed the right thing for me to do at that time in my life. My campaign slogan: THE RIGHT VOICE. THE RIGHT TIME.

I even met Hillary at a book signing in San Francisco and had the chance to speak to her. I told her I was running for Assembly, and she told me enthusiastically, "Win!"

ON THE CAMPAIGN TRAIL

The real experience of running for office is grueling. During the day-to-day, all-inclusive twenty-four-hour march of time spent raising money and being front-and-center everywhere you go—and on top of that trying to look your best—was challenging. My blazer collection went from a few to a closet full of different colors, not to mention matching pants, blouses, and shoes. For this LGBTQ woman, it was a journey trying to keep up the professional business look every single day. I was stepping outside of my comfort zone, but it was definitely worth it.

Running for office took on a life of its own. Fundraising, I discovered, was so important; data and polls were also critical, especially in a race like mine, and strong political connections were the key to maneuvering successfully through the system. Everything always came back to, *How much money have you raised? and Who is supporting you?*

Contacts? Connections? I had quite a few of those. Being a Delegate and president of a LGBTQ Democratic club, along with my contacts from the Hillary campaign, seemed to be a catalyst to opening numerous doors. I met Gavin Newsom, who was Lt. Governor of California at the time, when coordinating an event for him with my club. I threw a rally for congressional candidates and went to every function I could to network and collect business cards. I spent my time at the conventions and gatherings of Democratic leaders seeking to connect with—sometimes it felt like "stalking"—the Party leaders in order to obtain advice and leads. Their endorsements would result, I knew, in the opening of doors for additional resources, including critical funding opportunities.

One of my most noteworthy connections was Fiona Ma. A former assemblywoman, Fiona won her race for California State Treasurer as the first woman of color, receiving more votes than any of her predecessors. Fiona has turned out to be one of my greatest allies from day one and has continued to mentor me along the way. I am proud to call her my friend.

Being on the campaign trail meant a schedule full of house parties, phone time to raise money, and face-to-face meetings with as many influencers as possible. I'd attended every Democratic club meeting and function, and, always being asked to say a few words, developed my stump speech along the way.

I had a group of friends who volunteered to help my campaign but most of them worked full-time and could only help now and then. As the campaign started to kick into high gear, I realized I needed more help. Early on in the campaign, I was told that I needed a campaign/finance manager and an assistant. I was told to hire consultants. All these staff hires required money and were expensive for the campaign.

One of the smartest things I did, early in 2018, was to hire an assistant. The funds we raised paid for staffing, so she started out part-time, but I was able to promote her to full-time as the campaign kicked into high gear. She became my sidekick, holding my purse and collecting cards as I shook hands with people at events. Her capable presence helped me stay focused and organized as the campaign grew. She called volunteers, collected money for the treasurer, organized mailings, and just generally helped me stay on track.

Shortly thereafter, I hired a campaign manager. He was recommended to me by a consultant I had met, but I fired him after a month because he didn't perform as promised. I didn't hire a campaign manager after that experience. Instead, I took on the role of interim project leader myself. Our campaign performed fine without a manager, until the last two months, when I really felt the pain of not having a leader. At that point, a friend and mentor of mine, whom I'd met while working on the 2008 Hillary campaign and is a political force in her own right, came to stay with me for the last six weeks of the campaign and became the campaign leader so I could be the candidate. Many other dedicated volunteers also worked tirelessly to help when and where they could: from political strategy to canvassing day and night to field operations.

For the last five months of the campaign, I rented an office in a shopping center across the street from Sierra College in Rocklin, near my house. The location was perfect, not only to get student volunteers to assist in the campaign, but also to maintain a strong presence on campus to help win the Millennial vote. I decided that empowering my team of volunteers was my best strategy, and soon we formed a cohesive campaign team.

MEMORABLE MOMENTS

Running for office made me cry, laugh, and tested my patience. But some memories of the people I met and the places I visited will always stay in the front of my mind and remind me why I ran for office in the first place.

One six-year-old girl, Piper, would come to every local event. She would write me notes and come to the office, put stamps on postcards, and generally just be one of the best volunteers. She was a Girl Scout and a kindred spirit. Her adoration kept me going.

On the campaign trail, I always spoke about our seniors and how they are disenfranchised by skyrocketing drug prices and rent increases. One senior put seven one-dollar bills in a donation envelope after telling me she could hardly pay her rent on social security. She told me, "I believe in you." I will never forget those seven dollars.

I attended a UDW—United Domestic Workers—picnic at

Johnson Springview Park. The UDW union provides protection for caregivers and their patients. I heard story after story from the caregivers of how they live on the $440 per week they get from the state. I heard a story of a fifty-four-year-old woman who worked for American Airlines, had a stroke, and now her husband had to take care of her as a paraplegic in her wheelchair. They live on $440 a week. Or the mom who's thirty-four-year-old son is blind and she, too, is on the same assistance.

There are more stories to tell, but one thing I know for sure is that these are the reasons that will keep you going on the campaign trail, no matter how grueling it is, because these people are depending on you to represent their issues and to be their voice.

THE ELECTION

November 3rd was a strange day.

Deep down, I knew winning against the incumbent was a long shot. Our campaign did robocalls, commercials with Dolores Huerta on Telemundo, Latino radio, sent out over 12,000 handwritten postcards and 6,000 brochures, canvassed, phone banked, ran text campaigns, and put out over a thousand yard signs and large freeway signs. We were praised for running the best get-out-the-vote campaign. But was it all enough?

Our office was buzzing that night. Personal friends and campaign workers flew in from Seattle and drove in from the Bay Area. My dedicated volunteers were excited, but I was feeling so much stress behind my smiles. I didn't want to disappoint them when they had all worked so hard to get us to that night. We had beer and wine and a beautiful buffet, along with a TV that streamed the results. As it turned out, we didn't know what the final vote count was that night. We wouldn't know until weeks later. All I knew that night was that we had lost.

ELECTION DETOX

The day after the election, my opponent announced his victory and then, immediately, announced his run for an upcoming special election for our State Senate seat. Before the dust had even settled on our race, and before we knew the final vote count, he stated over social media that he was running for a different seat in a special election. This was, to put it mildly, frustrating and confusing.

The final count, weeks later, was 58 percent to 42 percent. I received almost 95,000 votes after having raised $200,000. For a first-time Democratic senior LGBTQ candidate, this was an historic feat, even if we didn't make it over the finish line.

People in the community were very supportive. "You'll get him next time," or "You ran the best campaign around!" or "You would've been a great in the Assembly," they told me. That last one got to me the most.

I took off with my partner to Bodega Bay for a few days to detox from the campaign. It felt as though someone in our family had died. I was in mourning. I was numb. As I watched my friends win their elections, I couldn't help but feel a little jealous.

RISING FROM THE ASHES

It took about three months to shake off the remnants of the campaign. I restarted my real estate business again and sold a couple houses. Now that I was considered an "Ex Officio" former candidate, I had votes with the California Democratic Party and appointed delegates for the party convention.

Running for office is very expensive, and I learned this the hard way during the 2018 run. The last two months of the campaign takes every penny out of the coffers you have painstakingly raised. We raised money but not enough for all the expenses to close out the coffers, so I, unexpectedly, had to pay $15,000 of my own money to our treasurer to close out my campaign committee. I learned that at the end of a campaign, surprises and expenses pop up. You don't realize what's happening until the dust settles.

In 2020, I decided to run again against the same opponent but with my eyes fixed directly on expenses and to plan better the second time around. But running this time was during

Covid I did run again for the Assembly against Kevin Kiley and it was quite different. There was no going to fundraisers, no meet-and-greet with voters—it was all online and I ran my campaign literally from my desk at home. I did raise $155,000. I did not hire staff this time except for my virtual assistant I hired in New Jersey. She helped me completely virtually with newsletters and social media. She even helped champion phone banks. But I saved so much money doing as much as I could myself from my desk. The unions and legislative support were my greatest donors as fundraising was difficult. I ended up only spending about $2000 of my own funds this second time and in the end I received 124,000 votes with 43 percent, but not enough to unseat Kevin Kiley in this red district.

CANDIDATE TARA SREEKRISHNAN

Office Sought: Cupertino City Council
District/Municipality: City of Cupertino
Population: 60,170
Opponents: Incumbent city council member, incumbent mayor, two school board members, former mayor of Cupertino, a community activist, and a business security consultant
Personal Info: Asian-American, twenty-five years old, city council aide

POLITICAL LANDSCAPE OF CUPERTINO

In 2018, eight candidates joined the race for three seats on the Cupertino City Council, including two incumbents, former mayors, and school board members. While most would assume a local election in a suburb that covers 11.3 square miles with fewer than 30,000 voters may well go overlooked, the Cupertino City Council election became a lightning rod for controversy and an emblem of the housing debate pervading cities across the Bay Area, big and small alike.

The election season saw competing billion-dollar development proposals, threats of multimillion-dollar lawsuits, the invocation of a new and highly controversial state law, four successful citizen ballot referendum petitions, hundreds of thousands of dollars in independent expenditures, explosive legal claims filed by city officials, and inescapable threats and attacks.

Elections can leave candidates and voters jaded and cynical. As a millennial, a first-time candidate, a progressive Democrat, and a woman of color, my campaign faced an uphill battle as we forged ahead to the finish line. What I learned from running is that even if you don't win the overall election, being on the ballot can, in and of itself, be worthwhile.

IN THE BEGINNING

Nestled near the foothills of the Santa Cruz Mountains, Cupertino is renowned as a hub of Silicon Valley innovation and home to one of the most successful technology companies in the world. From One Infinite Loop to the new "spaceship" campus, Apple Inc. has been headquartered in Cupertino since the company's incorporation in 1977. One of the most educated cities in California, Cupertino is a popular place to raise families thanks to the city's exceptional school system. A culturally diverse city, Cupertino is also rich in its remarkably overlooked politics, which are often of meaningful consequence.

I've lived in this city since I was five years old. As I grew up, my parents inspired my future public service through the ways in which they gave back to the community. Throughout my childhood, my mother, Anita, inspired me to believe in the values of public service through her own generous actions. She served the Cupertino public school system as a librarian, fundraiser, and volunteer organizer. She never sought recognition for the ways she served her community—instead, she just worked quietly in the background, doing what she did for the benefit of others.

My parents taught me to work hard in public school and give back to my community. I attended Murdock-Portal Elementary School, Kennedy Middle School, and Monta Vista High School. Given that I grew up in a minority-majority city—more than 60 percent of Cupertino is Asian—I never felt like an outsider, despite being a person of color. Our school system is also one of the most competitive and demanding in the state, with a strong focus on academics rather than social activities. As a result, students like me who graduated from Cupertino schools have been thoroughly prepared for leadership in every area of business, government, and society.

During those formative school years, certain teachers, authors, and social justice warriors played an important role in my formation as a political activist. My environmental science teacher in high school helped shape my worldview and sense of civic responsibility through deep dives into consumerism, corporate accountability (or lack thereof), and environmental sustainability. She also taught us how girls around the world have the power to uplift their communities when given access to adequate education. The work and writings of feminist authors inspired me to pursue justice and equality through political action and civic engagement. As a student, in addition to studying classical piano, I balanced several community service activities, including volunteering at Deer Hollow Farm and Sacred Heart Community Service, and raising money for educational programs in India.

Serving the greater good has been part of the fabric of my family, a perspective that has informed my life choices from a young age. Just as my parents brought me up in this great community, I hope to raise a family of my own here. I am enormously grateful for the privileges I've been afforded by being raised in such a unique city, and my mission is to ensure the same opportunities exist for others who want to thrive and succeed here as well—not just the wealthiest among us. I've lived in the area long enough to know that our biggest problems— from housing and transit to workers' rights—are regional, which means that even in a quiet suburb like Cupertino, we need relentless advocates who believe social justice, economic justice, and environmental justice must work in conjunction.

After high school, I attended Mills College in Oakland, the oldest women's college on the West Coast, where I studied classical music, education, women in politics, and political economy. I juggled teaching piano in Cupertino while completing my coursework. Straight out of college, I set out to work as a community organizer for local campaigns, including a local re-election campaign for my progressive Congressman. Inspired by the historic nomination of Hillary Rodham Clinton as the first female presidential candidate for a major party, I volunteered on her presidential campaign and was elected to serve as one of her delegates to the 2016 Democratic National Convention. I'm especially passionate about the work I have done to politically activate our high school and college students in Cupertino and the surrounding San Jose area through the several campaigns I have worked on.

My time as a legislative staffer for the City of Berkeley, a bastion of progressive politics and tolerance, was an enlightening and educational experience. I had the great fortune and opportunity to work for a progressive Berkeley councilwoman who continuously focused on policies and services directed toward helping the most disadvantaged. Berkeley City Council is one of the most progressive, proactive, and solutions-oriented legislative bodies in the state of California. During my time working for the city council, Berkeley reaffirmed its status as a sanctuary city, divested from President Trump's border wall, and took steps to sever ties with Wells Fargo due to unethical practices and investment in the Dakota Access Pipeline. These values ultimately stuck with me and helped shape my priorities and determination to make difficult decisions that benefit ordinary citizens and working-class families back home in Cupertino.

As a Berkeley City Council legislative staffer, I served many of the functions of a regular councilmember behind the scenes, which granted me a wealth of experience in what it takes to effectively govern and manage a city. I wanted to bring the tools, knowledge, and experience back to my own city with hopes that Cupertino City Council could be more proactive on certain areas I cared about, including housing, transit, and the environment.

While still working for the City of Berkeley, I initiated and advocated for several pieces of legislation to come in front of the Cupertino City Council, including additional housing at all income levels, but especially, more funds for affordable housing. Some legislation was even successfully implemented by the City of Cupertino. I also served on our Community Choice Aggregation (Silicon Valley Clean Energy) Citizens' Advisory Board; SVCE provides carbon-free electricity to Cupertino as our default option (as opposed to Pacific Gas and Electric).

I learned a wealth of information and political strategy from assuming leadership roles in environmental, progressive, and Democratic Party committees, conferences, and activist clubs that have galvanized my community behind action plans to address our historic housing crisis, combat climate change, implement neighborhood traffic mitigations and safety improvements, and even fight to save an emergency acute-care hospital critical to thousands, just to highlight a few.

WHY I RAN

As a campaign and legislative staffer, I enjoyed helping candidates and policymakers who had the capacity to truly improve people's lives, although I never planned to run for office myself. But like many folks of my generation across the country, I felt compelled by particularly pressing times, as we saw the profound ramifications of the Trump administration— the culmination of a growing far-right movement.

As right-wing extremism has bubbled up from the shadows, violence has ensued, such as the 2017 Berkeley protests when anti-Trump and neo-Nazi groups clashed near the UC-Berkeley campus and Berkeley Civic Center. During one of those events, I couldn't get to work, which was on lockdown as a result of the chaos at City Hall. In response to white nationalist bigotry, the City of Berkeley started a campaign in the form of window signs that spread like wildfire throughout the region, becoming Bay Area Stands United Against Hate. These movements inspired my sense of solidarity with likeminded people who similarly sought a more just, inclusive, and diverse society.

During my experience as a delegate at the 2016 Democratic National Convention, I witnessed how Hillary Clinton, the most qualified and competent presidential candidate, faced a disproportionate degree of scrutiny simply because she was a woman—and what's more, she lost to a corrupt, narcissistic misogynist facing multiple allegations of sexual misconduct. Following Trump's inauguration, tens of thousands of women around the country marched in protest. Then, in 2018, we ran for political office to reshape and reclaim our government so it works for ordinary people.

Whereas Cupertino council members rarely introduce legislation and council items themselves, while working for Berkeley City Council, I saw council members introduce several pieces of legislation at each meeting. I felt most frustrated by Cupertino's unproductive stance on housing. My boss in Berkeley, by contrast, led a successful charge to increase affordable housing funds and other housing initiatives.

I see young people like me, born to immigrant parents and raised in Cupertino, as well as our parents, grandparents, and others invested in our community, being priced out of Cupertino at an alarming rate. At twenty-five years old, I have had to work seventy-hour weeks, or hold two jobs at a time, since high school, in order to afford to continue living in the community in which I was raised. The millennial population has decreased drastically due to the soaring prices of rent and home ownership in Silicon Valley. Not unlike other cities across the Bay Area, the vast majority of new housing can be purchased for millions of dollars or rented for $3,000 to $5,000 per month.

Cupertino has been significantly below the affordable housing targets set by regional planning agency Association of Bay Area Governments (ABAG); even if all projects proposed during the 2014-2022 Regional Housing Needs Allocation (RHNA) cycle were built, Cupertino would meet only 3.4 percent of the goal for low- and very-low-income housing, 4.8 percent for moderate housing, and a comparatively higher 26 percent for above-moderate income housing.

Before running for city council, I advocated for increasing the Affordable Housing Mitigation Fee required in large, commercial office projects (not including small businesses), like the Apple "spaceship." These massive office projects have notoriously contributed very little to our affordable housing funds, considering the number of jobs they create. I pushed for the fee to go into a fund that would support the production of new and rehabilitated housing for lower-income and workforce ownership housing, including first-time homeownership opportunities, but the initiative went nowhere.

The burden of the housing crisis isn't just on the mid-range and lower-income residents of Cupertino; even the highest-paid professionals, people making two or three times more than the median income, cannot afford to live here. Teachers, firefighters, police officers, lower-income families, and young people don't even stand a chance. But the wellbeing of our community depends on the inclusion of all of these essential members of our society.

Cupertino's job growth has continued to outpace population growth; the number of jobs in Cupertino has grown 50 percent since the mid-2000s, and 90 percent of those workers commute into the city. Though job growth contributes to overall economic advancement for the region, it also augments our housing shortage.

Unfortunately, those of us concerned about the state of our community rarely feel heard in Cupertino City Council meetings. In meeting after meeting, our city council appeared to simply rubber-stamp whatever was put in front of them rather than thinking through issues critically and being proactive with the legislation they introduced. More often than not, it seemed like our political system had been taken over by inaccessible politicians and special interests working behind the scenes.

Despite my civic involvement in Cupertino and the surrounding area as a volunteer, there are too many roadblocks to effecting change from the outside, as opposed to being inside city governance. Given that the Cupertino City Council doesn't have staff, I knew the only way I could better serve Cupertino was to go beyond volunteering to running for a seat on city council.

As a campaign organizer and legislative staffer, I knew how to run campaigns and pass legislation. And frankly, I'd had enough of our local officials not taking seriously the issues that mattered most to me. So, I decided it was the perfect opportunity for me to take the plunge and run for office myself. I ran to bridge divides within the city council and bring the community together behind comprehensive solutions—the two extremely polarized sides of our community were destroying our quality of life.

What I didn't realize was just how wide and deep was that chasm, and how difficult it would be to bridge the divide.

ON THE CAMPAIGN TRAIL: A ONE-ISSUE ELECTION

While five of my opponents had already run successful campaigns in the area, some having been on ballots two, three, or even five times, I was starting from scratch. I began gathering my troops a year in advance of the 2018 midterms. While I formally filed my candidacy for Cupertino City Council the summer before the November elections, my team and I started knocking on doors as early as February. Running for city council soon became a full-time job that kept me on my feet and on my toes for months on end.

Each candidate for city council raised only about $20,000 to $50,000 individually, but independent expenditure PACs poured close to $1 million into the race. To put that in perspective, that's more than $25 per voter, compared to the $15.20 per voter nationwide it took to get Trump elected. Although my campaign didn't receive any independent expenditure funding, we were able to organize a passionate and dedicated team who raised more than $40,000, wholly from community members, often in small donations.

Without extensive funding for political mailers, the largest component of my campaign was the field campaign. My team included around 150 volunteers—many of whom were high school and college students eager to support a young candidate—who took shifts going door-to-door to talk to voters. Of Cupertino's 60,000 residents, 27,000 of them are eligible to vote. Our team knocked on about 13,000 doors—I knocked on about 2,000 doors myself.

My campaign's core concerns were affordable and adequate

housing, expanding our transit options, and protecting the environment through sustainable initiatives. Most of the other candidates had no concrete plans—just vague ideology—whereas I presented a better grasp of the issues and real plans for the city. Our message and efforts eventually earned us most of the major endorsements in the race, including from our local Democratic Party, the Sierra Club, every labor union in the county, our state senator, our state senate president, and our state controller.

Given my previous activism, I knew how to balance interests and create harmony with different stakeholders. What I soon discovered, however, was that Cupertino residents were myopically focused on one frustrating issue alone: the fate of the Vallco mall.

The saga involved two opposing entities: Cupertino City Council and Sand Hill Property Company, whose multibillion-dollar plan to redevelop the Vallco mall, a blighted and empty shopping center in the heart of Cupertino, has led to intense divisions in our community. What ultimately gets built there will have a profound impact on our future. Cupertino City Council's leadership has failed to act decisively to protect the community's needs, and at the time of this writing, it remains unclear whether something meaningful will ever be built within the empty, haunting halls of a once thriving community space.

Sand Hill purchased the Vallco mall for some $320 million dollars. In terms of investment, the development partnership hit the jackpot in buying more than fifty acres of prime real estate in the heart of Silicon Valley, just steps from Apple's new megacampus. Sand Hill has played politics for six years, surviving highly contentious campaigns and ballot initiatives and promising utopian Vallco projects—one iteration even included the largest green roof in the world—to finally get city approval of almost two million square feet of highly lucrative office space at the Vallco site in September of 2018.

As I repeated throughout my campaign, the people of Cupertino and the Bay Area need more housing and affordable housing options now more than ever; it is key to inclusivity and fairness in our city. While Sand Hill has promised to build housing and some retail alongside their sprawling office space, they have never been upfront about how so much planned office space would exacerbate the imbalance between jobs and housing in Cupertino, a ratio that drives displacement, carbon emissions, and local and regional housing prices. It's not Sand Hill's responsibility to look out for the interests of the community—it's City Hall's.

In early 2018, Sand Hill sought to expedite its long-desired revival of the Vallco mall space, using a new streamlining process under a well-intentioned new law, Senate Bill 35, in conjunction with the normal city development approval process. The previous council majority placed no reasonable limits on the amount of office space to be built at Vallco and even secured for the developer a sweetheart deal featuring 1.75 million square feet of office space.

I participated in numerous public forums in which I expressed my belief that while we should applaud efforts to create housing in a time where market-rate housing costs increasingly soar, our problems are regional. This means that we must always consider our place within a greater environment when approaching any policies that may have profound effects for years to come. When the great majority of our daytime residents are commuting from outside our city, we should be concerned about any plan which further exacerbates our housing deficit.

Sand Hill took out a political insurance policy to protect their investment. They utilized the power granted by the Supreme Court's infamous Citizens United case to spend unlimited sums of money in independent expenditures (disguised under seemingly innocuous labels like "Cupertino Getting Things Done Together") to reward those who voted to support them in the past and to fill vacant council seats with those friendly to their interests: close to one million dollars in a relatively small electorate with only about 27,000 registered voters.

Compounding the appearance of corruption, Cupertino's former city attorney filed an explosive claim against the city, claiming that the council fired him for questioning the legality of the streamlined Vallco proposal and that a councilman threatened him with retaliation unless he supported the proposal. These assertions were the beginning of a multimillion-dollar lawsuit, which, regardless of the outcome, will squander taxpayer dollars that could be used to mitigate traffic, expand transportation, and address climate change.

As happens in any election, major stakeholders invested time, money, and power to sway residents to vote according to their interests, including the Cupertino Chamber of Commerce, Sand Hill Corp., environmental groups, labor unions, and Better Cupertino, a grassroots network of Cupertino residents known for fighting previous iterations of Vallco they deemed too massive for the city. Every day of the campaign, voters were bombarded by vicious attack ads in the form of nasty mailings, flyers, emails, lawn signs, billboards, and even tractor trailers from the two opposing sides.

Of the eight candidates in the race for Cupertino City Council, three were slated against the Vallco development, and three were for the developer-supported Vallco plan. I found myself stuck in the middle, a lone voice advocating reason between these two extremely polarized sides. As a candidate who wanted to see more housing in the city built in a sustainable way, there was no clear path to victory.

Two months before election day, the election and the city were taken over by two concurrent Vallco development proposals, contentious competing lawsuits, and a citizen's ballot referendum organized by Better Cupertino.

Better Cupertino knew what residents wanted to hear, and, more importantly, they knew what the community feared— namely, the loss of the small town they loved as Cupertino grew into a large urban center.

Although I had issues with the developer's Vallco proposal, I told the good folks at Better Cupertino that I could not support the referendum. It's easy to collect signatures and get the community fired up against a plan; it's much harder to get the community to rally behind a plan that can actually be implemented. I was afraid that without a feasible alternative, which should include a sufficient amount of housing, the referendum would not be productive. After years of failed proposals and woefully non-inclusive community discussion, I believed it was time to finally get this right.

While I continue to look to the community for guidance on issues such as this, I subscribe to the philosophy that leaders, and those running for leadership positions, need to present a socially responsible vision to their community and proactively pursue strategies to build toward that vision. Yes, we should critically examine proposals to illuminate any deficiencies, but we must work together to come up with forward-looking solutions, not just revert to obstruction. While new housing will always bring new challenges, my goal was to best address these challenges; experts agreed that stalling housing would further exacerbate our challenges long-term, and I could not in good conscience support proposals that didn't adequately account for this urgent need, even if it meant losing support from my community and the overall election.

MEMORABLE MOMENTS

Though my campaign for city council had its share of ups and downs, several moments in particular stand out from the rest. One of the earliest was the controversy that ensued after I wrote an op-ed for *San Jose Inside*, published on July 29, 2018, entitled, "Cupertino City Council Should Hold Apple Corporation Financially Accountable."

In my piece, I weighed in on an ongoing debate in our community about the level of contribution Apple should be making toward alleviating our housing and infrastructure issues. To the outside world, Cupertino is probably best known as home to one of the most innovative companies in history, bringing 23,000 jobs to Cupertino alone. After twenty-four years on One Infinite Loop, Apple built a brand-new, five-billion-dollar campus—a round building a mile wide nicknamed "the spaceship"—increasing space for an ever-growing workforce.

At the same time, however, the influx of employees has created chronic traffic that has put incredible strain on our roads, intersections, and transit system. Cupertino is not yet connected to our larger transit systems, including VTA or BART, and thus most folks commute in single-occupancy vehicles. The community had been discussing the possibility of a tax on Apple to support funds for Cupertino's infrastructure, which the majority of residents who responded to polls supported. I wrote the op-ed ahead of the city council's consideration of this ballot measure.

The backlash was strong and immediate.

Apple's government relations executive emailed a councilmember a one-word message: "Really?!" Though this councilmember had been supportive of my previous advocacy efforts, they suggested I walk back my statements and keep my honest opinions to myself before election day. Eventually, the city council backed down to Apple, and the potential tax was tabled indefinitely.

While campaigning, I also caught a lot of flak for my age.

One of my mother's many community activities has been co-chairing the annual fundraiser for the Fremont Union High School District (FUHSD) Foundation, which in 2018 was a crab feed, known as the best-attended non-festival event in Cupertino. At the close of the event, one of my opponents, who served on the crab feed committee alongside my mother, approached her alone in the parking lot.

"Your daughter shouldn't be in this race," my opponent told her. "I think she's making a big mistake. It's not her time. These issues are too important."

It wasn't the first time I'd heard innuendos that I was too young to be running for city council, but I was taken aback that my opponent would go so far as to say such a thing to my own mother.

The overwhelming majority of voters in Cupertino are in their mid-forties and above, and all my opponents were about twice my age or older. In their minds, running for city council is something you do after you've had a lifelong career; perhaps it's simply a status symbol. Some folks thought of me as an "entitled millennial" who didn't "deserve" to be on the city council—these people held the same mentality toward their property values and allowing outsiders into our community. Their attitude: "I worked hard to get here, so why do you deserve to live here?" My campaign theme of the benefits of inclusion and diversity was lost on this segment of the population. The millennial population in Cupertino and our greater region continues to dissipate; younger families struggle to afford to live here or enter our school system, which has led to declining enrollment and major budget shortfalls. Folks my age don't have an adequate voice in the issues, which will continue to affect us years from now.

In a Facebook post on June 23, 2017, Alexandria Ocasio-Cortez, who was twenty-eight when she ran for Congress, noted she'd experienced something similar: "I have been told to wait my turn; that I'm not savvy enough, connected enough, experienced enough." My age had nothing to do with the depth of my convictions and readiness to serve my constituents. For every person who said, "You're too young. You're my daughter's age," and slammed the door in my face, there were plenty of others who were inspired by my youth, energy, and drive to move the needle on issues that mattered to all of us.

Even if insiders on both sides would have preferred that I'd stayed out of the race altogether, many Cupertino residents were happy to see a fresh face on the ballot. I participated in several public forums to debate my opponents, some of which were hosted by the Rotary Club, the League of Women Voters, and the Chamber of Commerce. At an informal forum organized by a neighborhood group, I felt like the only adult in the room as three of the candidates took polarized sides against the other three. For more than two hours, my opponents, driven by their respective ideologies and deep-seated resentment, talked over one another in combative tones, while I tried to express what I hoped to accomplish in a clear, levelheaded way.

At the end, I figured no one in attendance had heard a word I'd said amid so much noise. But just as I walked out, a woman from the audience came up to me. "I'm supporting you," she told me with a wink.

To my surprise, several other people who had been in the audience at that forum told me the same thing in the following days. Even when I thought I'd been drowned out by all these older, more experienced people fighting throughout the debate, my candidacy had been respected and appreciated more than I realized. Unfortunately, very few Cupertino residents watched the public forums or saw all the candidates next to each other, and as a first-time candidate, despite knocking on 2,000 doors, I couldn't have as many one-on-one interactions with people in the city to allow them to hear what I had to say.

A significant part of my platform was that I was a clean-money candidate—no donations from corporations, especially not from developers, given the centrality of the Vallco issue. I also created and signed a pledge to renounce outside money spent on my behalf from corporate PACs. Despite this overt stance, rumors began to spread that corporate developers were funding my campaign. My volunteers canvassing neighborhoods heard from supporters who believed these widespread whisper attacks.

"They were supporting you," volunteers explained, "but then they heard from a friend that you were funded by developers. So, they removed our campaign signs from their front lawns."

It didn't matter that the rumors were a complete lie—between the "pro-development" slate and the "anti-development" slate, I ended up caught in the crossfire.

THE ELECTION

In many ways, the election was over before election day, thanks to Better Cupertino's successful efforts at pushing a citywide referendum on the Vallco proposal. Their supporters knocked door-to-door, stood outside the library, and held meet-and-greets around town in support of a referendum, which served as a pedestal for their candidates at the same time.

About 20 percent of Cupertino residents held strong feelings about stopping development, while the other 80 percent of voters followed an intense force of word-of-mouth for the Better Cupertino slate, which spread through WhatsApp, Nextdoor, and other neighborhood networks and pervaded our small city. In just thirty days, they gathered more than 5,000 signatures—an incredible feat for any organization. It demonstrated not only how well-organized and connected the political action committee was, but also how the entire city seemed to vote according to a herd mentality.

In the end, the newly elected city council voted to accept the referendum rather than take it to a public election.

Even before election day, it was clear that public sentiment was behind the Vallco referendum. Among the 27,000 eligible voters within Cupertino, the three councilors who won the election—all candidates running on the anti-development slate—received about 7,000 to 8,000 votes.

By contrast, I only won about 5,000 votes. A lot of people I met said they voted for me because they saw that I was the most levelheaded candidate in the race. Most folks outside of Cupertino would agree that the two polarized sides were wrong. You don't allow a corporation to decide how a city is developed, but at the same time, you don't want to be unproductive and simply block housing across the board when we need it so urgently.

On election day, the votes came in around 8:00 p.m., but due to an extremely close tie between two people, the official tally wasn't announced until a month later after an official recount. I stayed out of the drama because I knew from the signatures on the referendum that I'd already lost, which I confirmed on the registrar of voters' website.

ELECTION DETOX

A few nights later, I made concession calls to my opponents, one of whom knew very little about the job of a city council member. When I brought up the recent transient occupancy tax, or hotel tax, that the city council had passed on short-term rentals like Airbnb, they didn't even know what Airbnb was. With residents decrying the state of Cupertino housing, they should have known not only what Airbnb was but how landlords have turned whole apartment buildings into short-term rentals, further reducing the availability of rental housing for permanent residents. It frustrated me to see people elected to our city council who only wanted to be able to vote "no" on a single issue without having a vested interest in the good of the community as a whole.

Though I was incredibly proud of the race I'd run, I was also relieved once the campaign was over because I had been working twelve-hour days for months. Just having been part of the race made me stand out among the people who knew me. At family gatherings, my friends and family members wanted to rant about politics, whereas I hoped for a break from it all. Since I became involved in politics, Thanksgiving has never been the same!

Perhaps the worst part of losing was being on the receiving end of so many condolences. That part can be difficult to endure.

RISING FROM THE ASHES

One of the hardest lessons I learned from running for city council was how people tend to make irresponsible decisions at the voting booth. The election of Donald Trump proves this point well enough, but I witnessed the same myopic vision in our local community. Many people focus only on their personal interests, fears, and assumptions, while failing to see the bigger picture of how a deteriorating community at large could affect those same self-interests.

As a candidate, I also realized the consequence of not

picking a side, especially in the midst of a contentious debate. Ideology on either side of the fence is dangerous if you're not applying pragmatism. Americans across the country tend to get so polarized around ideologies that we can't get anywhere because people aren't willing to consider what works in real life for the greater good of a community. I entered my race as the pragmatic, reasonable candidate centered between two extremely contentious slates. Political races and discourse tend to be quite emotional, and reason often gets lost in the fog.

Many people who lose their campaigns for public office feel so jaded by the entire experience that they bow out of civic engagement. But like the other women featured in this book, I plan to stay involved in the issues that inspired me to run in the first place.

The Vallco redevelopment issue is likely to drag on for years to come. Though I feel my community cannot effectively tackle existential issues such as housing and climate change at the city level alone, I plan to invest my energy at the county and state levels to address the same issues I ran on. Shortly after the election, I accepted a new job at our County government with a County Supervisor who was also running to represent Cupertino and much of our County in the California State Senate. He won and I now have the opportunity to continue my work on the issues I care about at the state level.

As I sit down to write this, three years since the election, I have remained on the nonprofit boards and progressive committees I'd volunteered for previously, while also joining new ones, such as one that has been fighting to hold accountable a huge industrial polluter right in our backyard. Most recently, I was appointed to fill a vacancy for another local public office. I currently serve as a Trustee on our County's Board of Education, and I will be on the ballot again in 2022.

It is an honor to continue my service to the community as a Trustee where I'm able to put our students and younger generation first and do what's best for them. And it doesn't escape me for one moment that the relationships I built and lessons I learned during my campaign in 2018 led me to this position.

The campaign gave me many opportunities to be a humble, thoughtful listener to the views and needs of all sides of an issue, especially those that spark passionate debate, in order to try to put forward solutions that can benefit everyone involved, which is critical to doing a good job as a public official.

I'm encouraged to know that countless young girls across Cupertino saw my campaign—a young Indian American woman and Monta Vista grad running for political office—as an example of the possibilities for their own future, whether as a volunteer, activist, or elected official.

We need bright young minds—especially women—ready to secure a brighter future for the next generation. My hope is that more and more women of all ages and backgrounds will pick up the mantle in their communities, learning from my and others' mistakes, so together we can evolve the way Americans engage with each other within political and civic milieus. Even if such a candidate doesn't win, her presence on the ballot gives voters the chance to do the right thing—to vote for someone who desires to serve her community and look out for the interests of everyone, not just a select few.

Candidate Myel Jenkins

Office Sought: School Board Trustee
District/Municipality: San Juan Unified School Board (Sacramento County)
Population: More than 200,000 voters covering seventy-two square miles of Sacramento County
Incumbent: One incumbent running for a second term with two seats open on the Board
Personal Information: Age forty-seven at time of election, Myel is bi-racial, divorced, with two children who attend San Juan schools.

Political Landscape of San Juan

San Juan Unified School District (SJUSD) covers seventy-two square miles of Sacramento County and serves students and families that live in the county's suburbs. Currently, it is the eleventh largest school district in California and has sixty-four schools that serve 40,000 students.

San Juan has a history of competitive elections. There are more than 200,000 voters within the San Juan district, and it is not uncommon for the top candidates in SJUSD races to win by securing 25,000 votes or more.

There were two seats up for election in 2018. One incumbent was running for re-election and the second incumbent decided to not run. The two school board trustees serving in the two seats that were up were white men who were older, retired with no children attending San Juan schools at the time. The 2018 election would shake up the makeup of the school board; with only one incumbent running, the outcome was guaranteed to bring in at least one new member who would be a woman, a person of color, and younger than most of the other school board trustees.

The November 2018 race was remarkable for the San Juan

Unified School District in many ways. One was that all four candidates were Democrats, including the incumbent, even though school board races are non-partisan. Even in non-partisan races, local political clubs can support candidates and provide endorsements that they then share with their membership and local voters; donate to endorsed candidates providing funds that can be used to purchase advertising to reach voters; and/or encourage club members to volunteer for the candidate by making phone calls or knock-on doors to get out the vote. The incumbent and three candidates, including me, were all Democrats seeking endorsements and donations from local Democratic clubs. In a school board race with four candidates and two seats, we were competing for club resources that included endorsements, donations, and volunteers.

The second remarkable piece of this particularly competitive race was that the three non-incumbent candidates, including me, were all women of color with kids attending San Juan schools. While there is a history of women running for seats on the San Juan school board, very few of those candidates were women of color running in a district in which their children were enrolled. Before the 2018 election, in fact, it had been over fifteen years since an elected school board member fit all of these characteristics: a woman, a person of color, and a parent with children in San Juan schools. And no seated school board trustees at the time of the 2018 election had any children attending San Juan schools.

WHY I RAN

I have had many roles over my life. I am a daughter, a sister, an athlete, a friend, a manager, a coach, a volunteer, a bi-racial woman, a wife, and my favorite: mom to my two sons, Dominic and August. My roles have shifted over the years, with some becoming less relevant and others becoming more prominent as my family and career grew. Some days I switch roles depending on the time of day.

Yet, there is one role that I never pictured trying on:

candidate. I have never harbored life-long political aspirations, dreamed of running for office at a young age, taken political science classes, or even volunteered on a political campaign until I became a candidate myself.

I always thought if you run for office and serve as an elected official, it is because you have nurtured long-term political ambitions, have far-reaching social networks, and access to capital to make funding a successful campaign attainable. These ideas around running for office never matched my own image of who I am or who I wanted to be.

And still, the thought of running for school board slowly creeped into my consciousness. It started as a small seed of an idea that gradually took root until I had to recognize it and respond to it.

I am one of those parents who can't help but to raise my hand to volunteer. That's how I became a soccer coach for my son's team for six years. That's how I became a Sunday School teacher at my parish for four years. I have always been compelled to say, "Yes, I can help."

My start as a parent volunteer began when my eldest son Dominic started kindergarten and I was able to volunteer weekly in his classroom. My volunteerism grew as each of my boys went up a grade level; I began volunteering in both classes once my youngest son started school and expanded my school involvement when I became active with the Parent Teacher Association (PTA). When the boys were in fifth and second grades, it became harder to find time in the workday to volunteer in the classroom. My workload gradually expanded, eliminating my capacity to be in the classroom on a regular basis. I still wanted to serve and be engaged, so I found a way to volunteer within my time limitations. Working with my son's school principal, I became our school's representative on the Superintendent Parent Advisory Committee, a school district-wide committee. I was happy to say yes and attend the once-a-month meetings to learn about district initiatives, share updates about our school and report back to the school principal on district news. It was at one of these committee meetings when I heard about the district's Local Control Accountability (LCAP) Parent Advisory Committee. The district was launching this committee to engage the community and advise how to allocate state funds on a local level to better support student achievement. I knew that I wanted to join this committee. As a mom of color volunteering in the classroom and serving on district committees, I did not often see other parents who looked like me or had similar experiences and saw this an opportunity to bring forth my perspective to help shape district initiatives and policies. That was it—I ended my term on the Superintendent Parent Advisory Committee after several years and I joined the (LCAP) Parent Advisory Committee in the first year that it was established.

The idea to run came to me one evening while attending one of these LCAP committee meetings, prompted by a presentation that I had heard a number of times over the years—one highlighting the academic achievement gaps of student groups by demographic breakdowns. And the data once again showed a significant achievement gap between the African American students in our district and their classmates.

I had seen similar data, presented in past meetings, that acknowledged this achievement gap, but I had yet to hear how our district programs were effectively addressing these differences and ensuring that all students, especially our African American students, were given the support and opportunities needed to academically succeed. Plans were in place, but the data showed that our district needed consistent, culturally appropriate strategies in order to make significant improvements.

That presentation, and all the ones that preceded it, made me realize we were stuck. It was then that I experienced the first flutter-thought: Sitting on this committee is not enough. I want to do more. I want to make a difference. I want to be on the school board.

I sat with the idea to run for school board for a year. It was a thought I would revisit continuously when reviewing district data and talking through education strategies at the LCAP Parent Advisory Committee meetings. The longer I thought about running, the more certain I became that I needed to take the leap. In November 2017, I realized that I needed to convert my ideas into action and prepare to run for school board in the November 2018 election.

ON THE CAMPAIGN TRAIL

There is nothing comparable to life on the campaign trail. It is everything you hear about and so much more. Running a campaign is grueling but dynamic, fast-paced but energizing, relentless but rewarding.

My life on the campaign trail evolved from the time I quietly decided in November 2017 that I would run, to each following month as the November 2018 election drew closer and closer. In my career I have worked in nonprofits, county government, and foundation settings, and my positions have ranged from manager to program planner, to my current role, director. I decided to approach campaigning as I would approach any new initiative at work—begin with research and develop an action plan and implement the plan using the project management skills that I have honed throughout my career.

I started my research with what I know—that is my network from volunteering, parenting, and working. I grabbed a pen and notebook and began mapping my network to identify who in my multiple circles was knowledgeable about running for office. My son August even joined me. He had just turned twelve and was curious about what it meant for me to run for office. I gave him a quick tutorial and let him know that it would take a lot of time, focus, and fundraising. He quietly left the room and came back with a notebook, a pen, and my cell phone. He then opened up my phone and started writing. Curious, I looked over to see what he was doing—he was doing his own mapping, fundraising mapping. My son, a political novice, was making notes of who I knew, pulling contacts from my phone and identifying who I should ask to donate to my campaign.

Seeing him voluntarily take on this task was confirmation that my family was all in and was supporting my run for office.

In doing the mapping, I realized that even though I was new to politics, I volunteered and worked with people who had political experience. My first call was to an old co-worker and friend who had experienced working on political campaigns. She then helped me to identify local political consultants, and from there I scheduled informational interviews with two consultants. In these meetings, I got quick tutorials about crafting campaign strategies specific to school boards. I learned that school board races are considered "down ballot" races and as local campaigns, the strategies to run for school board differ from strategies for running for a county seat or state office. We discussed how much I would need to fundraise to run a competitive race and landed on the fundraising goal of $25,000—enough funds to be able to purchase marketing that would reach the many thousands of voters in the San Juan Unified School District.

I continued with my research and reached out to a retired lobbyist who I had met when we both served on the board of directors for a local nonprofit. We met on a cold morning over steaming mugs of tea, and she talked candidly about the politics of running for office, the challenges of being a woman in the "old boys' network" of politics and the sacrifices it would take to stay focused on the campaign and fundraise while working full time and parenting. It was intimidating, but I remained inspired to run as a parent voice in our district; I felt ready for the challenge.

My next informational interview took place on a sunny afternoon over cups of coffee with a San Juan Unified School Board trustee who was serving her second term of office. We had met a few years prior, when I had served on the LCAP Parent Advisory Committee and she had participated as the board member representative. It was from her that I first learned about the opportunities to be endorsed by local Democratic clubs and the importance of completing endorsement questionaries. But it was also in this conversation that I got to ask my burning question: "Is it realistic for me to serve as a school board member and meet the multiple obligations I face as a working mom?" And it was she who reassured me that while governing was a huge time commitment, with intention and care, I could serve, be a mom, and work. That was the final element I needed to feel assured that I could run for school board. Again, it felt intimidating, but I felt up to the challenge, knowing that my husband was supportive and that my parenting time was shifting as my boys aged—the oldest was in high school and the youngest would be entering middle school the following year. This conversation was a good reminder that running for office while working full time and parenting would be tough, but it could be done.

I was as ready as I ever could be. Now it was time for me to act and begin building my campaign and my campaign team. As a political novice, I wanted help and guidance and knew that I couldn't do everything myself. In December 2017, I added two paid consultant positions to my campaign—a campaign consultant and a campaign treasurer.

I reconnected with one of the campaign consultants that I interviewed previously and brought him on as my consultant. It would still be a grassroots campaign, but I would have a consultant who could provide guidance on campaign strategies, help me understand voter data, develop a get-out-the-vote strategy, and connect me to other campaign services providers, like local printers. With my tight campaign budget, the consultant would provide campaign expertise on a limited basis, as opposed to hiring a campaign manager who would develop strategy and manage campaign tasks while working as a full-time paid staff.

I also hired a female-owned company to act as my campaign treasurer. Having a treasurer meant that I had an experienced firm to file all necessary campaign paperwork and reports with the county and state, so that I could be sure to stay in compliance with campaign laws. It meant that my campaign bank account was opened and managed, and my campaign expenses and fundraising were tracked as required by law. Having a paid treasurer gave me peace of mind, knowing that my campaign was following campaign laws, which allowed me to stay focused on campaign strategy, not compliance reporting.

All of these were required steps to build a solid foundation for a spring campaign announcement.

Now that my campaign foundation was in place, it was time to start my fundraising efforts to prepare for my campaign announcement. January 2018 became my time to practice fundraising and to get more comfortable with the "ask." I started small and went to family and my mentors—executive directors and supervisors that I worked under when I started my career in my twenties, to my most recent supervisor. My family gave the first donations, with my stepmom and my mother and father in-law giving generously, while my mom secured my first $1000 donation from her dear friend! My family's support made me more confident when calling and emailing my mentors with the announcement I was running for school board. I made individual asks, asking if they would support my candidacy to be a parent voice in support of the success of all students and be an early donor to my campaign. Each mentor was responsive and gave individually between $200 and $500, providing resources that I could use to launch my efforts. With early funds I was able establish my campaign messaging by preparing a campaign website and printing hundreds of "walk pieces" in advance of my February 2018 launch. I invested the initial donations to hire a web designer and, with the expertise of a close friend who is a graphic designer, drafted the walk piece for printing to have ready to give to voters when attending campaign events.

At the same time, I went back to my network and asked additional friends to help me prep for my February launch. I started with my friend who had helped months earlier with my first informational interview. We began to meet regularly on Sunday afternoons, setting up in my dining room with our laptops, typing a campaign project timeline and action steps, creating an event plan for a February campaign kick-off party, and developing the language for my website. We brought in one of my oldest and dearest high school friends, who is a talented graphic designer. The three of us met on weekends, rotating between meeting in my home and in coffee shops, each of us with a laptop fired up as we rapidly brainstormed, taking notes. We worked diligently through January, looking at websites from past local campaigns for inspirations, debating between draft campaign logos, and building out my Facebook campaign page.

I juggled the January weekend campaign-brainstorming meetings with planning for two spring campaign events. As a grassroots campaign I pulled in a set of friends to help put these events in motions. With my close friend from the neighborhood, we planned a February "kick off" party to introduce me to the local community as a candidate for the San Juan Unified School District. She graciously agreed to host the party, and we got to work drafting an invite list that included neighbors, PTA parents, friends from our kids' sports and school communities, and teachers from the neighborhood schools.

While planning the February launch, I was also working with my friend, the retired lobbyist, to host my first fundraiser event which would be held in April at her home. While the invitation list for the February launch drew heavily from my network as a parent and school volunteer, the invitation list for the April fundraiser drew more from my professional network in Sacramento area nonprofits and foundations. The fundraiser list included current and former colleagues from work, board members and executive directors of local non-profits, and past superintendents and board members of the San Juan Unified School District. The event was not until April, but we knew I only had one chance to make a first impression to voters and donors, and we wanted the impression to be that I was a viable and compelling candidate who was committed to the success of all students in San Juan.

By the time I officially announced in February, I had invested hours of time and energy in my campaign while continuing to work full time and parent my two sons. I was not alone in my prep work, a close group of friends helped to give me a strong start. Each of these friends generously donated their expertise and talents and some even the use of their homes. Because of this generosity, I didn't have to use donated funds to pay for graphic design services, catering, or space for campaign events; these "in-kind" donations were invaluable to my ability to move my grassroots campaign forward. The support from my family was also invaluable and allowed me to devote my time and energy to the start of my campaign, knowing that my family was committed. My husband took on more of the evening chauffeuring to and from evening sports events and my boys were cheering me on while I hit the campaign trail.

Once I announced my campaign, I was off and running and not looking back! My campaign gradually grew into a schedule that started when my alarm went off at five a.m. in the morning and ended when I went to bed at eleven p.m. or later. My early morning workouts were replaced by early morning emails, tracking incoming donations, writing thank you notes to donors, drafting a social media post for the day, and organizing the details of upcoming house parties hosted by my supporters. I would take forty-five minutes to organize my campaign for the day, and then I would switch gears and become mom again, getting ready for work and jumping in the car by 7:15 a.m. to drop off one son at his high school and the other at his elementary school.

I used my lunch hour for a variety of activities; rarely did lunchtime equal a break. I would shut my door and eat at my desk while making fundraising calls, strategizing with my campaign consultant, connecting with community influencers—like local elected officials—or catching up on campaign-related emails. I was committed to raising $25,000 to ensure that I had the funds to reach thousands of voters through printed walk pieces, digital advertising, and lawn signs. Continuously fundraising was critical to reaching this goal, so I used my lunch time to reach out to the network I had built through volunteering in the school community, serving as a board member of a local nonprofit, and my professional network of colleagues and mentors to invest in my campaign and donate.

Even when I left work at the end of the day, my day wasn't over. Evening became a time to attend local Democratic club meetings or house parties hosted in my honor. If I was not out in the community in the evening, there was a good chance that I was on my laptop at home writing responses to the various endorsement questionnaires from the Democratic clubs. And there were times when I couldn't pack everything into a regular day. I used vacation days in the spring to visit my school district, meet with the department directors, and visit school campuses. It was important that I could successfully fundraise and connect with our Democratic clubs to demonstrate that I was a viable candidate. It was equally important to continue to learn more about our San Juan School District as a candidate for school board.

Managing all aspects of the campaign while working full-time and parenting was challenging. I was on go from the time I started my day to when I went to bed. There was never enough time for the things I loved, like long family dinners, weekend workouts, or connecting with friends. But I made it work, day by day, by remembering that campaigning would not last forever.

Campaigning increased in intensity just after the July elections. The local Democratic clubs started to turn their focus toward the November election, which meant that the endorsement process was in full swing.

Even in a non-partisan race, such as a school board election, political endorsements can help propel a candidate forward by getting support from political clubs. Once a club chooses to endorse a candidate, they can provide a financial donation, offer their support by reaching out to their voters on behalf of the endorsed candidate, and recruit and organize campaign volunteers. Political clubs want to vet candidates before deciding to support their campaign and usually ask candidates to complete a questionnaire, participate in an interview hosted by a sub-committee of the club, or deliver a short speech to the club membership. Once those steps are taken, the club usually votes on which candidates they choose to endorse for their race. Seeking an endorsement represents a considerable investment of time and effort by the candidate.

The Democratic endorsement process for the San Juan Unified School District Board race—with four Democratic candidates, but only two seats up for election—was competitive. For me, the endorsement process was an emotional roller-coaster. There were a few endorsements where, despite my best effort, I was not selected as the endorsed candidate. Those times were often the most difficult in an already emotionally draining process. I would ground myself with the reminder that I had given it my best, but that the club determined that my viewpoint and goals were not the best fit for them. It always helped to take a deep breath, to remind myself to be grateful for the opportunity and to continue to move forward. Having a rocking playlist on my iPod ready with my favorite Beyonce songs always helped me to pick up my pieces and keep going!

There were also times, many in fact, when I was the endorsed candidate. And those times were thrilling. Receiving an endorsement, especially one that came with a campaign contribution, made me feel like I was on the top of the rollercoaster, that I was on the highest of highs. An endorsement always felt like validation, that there are voters who agreed that I was the best candidate to serve on the school board.

As we inched closer to election day, the weekends were increasingly filled with house parties to coordinate and attend, community fairs to participate in, and neighborhood walks to talk with voters. My reach had to spread to connect with as many voters as possible in the seventy-two square miles of our school district. I needed help to make that happen, and I asked an old colleague to take on the critical role of volunteer coordinator. With her assistance, we were able to bring on additional volunteers and use the weekends to reach the many voters of San Juan Unified.

Rolling into October, it was normal to have three or more

events each day, in addition to walking neighborhoods and knocking on doors. This was the most exhausting time of the campaign, and it was also the most exhilarating. Because our school district is so large it is difficult to know the dynamics of each neighborhood. Walking neighborhoods gave me the chance to meet students and parents in our district that I would not normally interact due to the large geographic span. I enjoyed the new experience of campaigning; it was energizing to see and learn more about the different parts of our community. I was also energized by meeting parents, teachers, and students, and hearing about what was important to them. I learned through walking neighborhoods and talking to students, families, and voters how much I enjoy connecting with people. This was a full grassroots campaign powered by a vision with the support of a solid team of volunteers willing to make it happen.

Memorable Moments

I was motivated to run for school board to bring my voice, a parental voice, to the table and to continue to bring attention to the opportunity gaps within our district. My hardest campaign struggles, however, came when my campaign commitments were in direct conflict with being a mom, and I had to put a number of family traditions on hold. For years, it has been a weekly tradition for me to bake cookies with August. During campaigning, I replaced baking cookies with drafting programs for upcoming fundraising parties. Instead of coaching Saturday soccer games, I attended endorsement interviews. Back-to-school nights for my sons were replaced by candidate forums; cheering Dominic at Friday night high school football games became speaking at community events. I missed participating in our family traditions, but I also knew that I would be campaigning for a finite amount of time.

One of my most memorable conflicts came in May. I was at work in my office when my cell phone rang. It was the school calling—a number that always made me nervous when it appeared on my phone in the middle of the school day. A month earlier, I had received a call from August's sixth-grade teacher. My son had had an allergic reaction to a bee sting and was being transported by ambulance to the hospital. Fortunately, he recovered quickly but now he needs to have an EpiPen on hand, and I'm left with a residual nervousness whenever I see the school's number pop up on my phone.

This call, too, was about August—he'd had a PE mishap and was being examined by paramedics for a possible concussion and broken finger. I was relieved that even though August required medical care, the incident was not serious enough to need ambulance transportation. I spent a few minutes at my desk juggling calls to his pediatrician before driving to the school and then to the orthopedic surgeon. The afternoon was busy with X-rays, a temporary wrap, and then scheduling appointments for additional X-rays and the cast. By the end, we had spent several hours at the doctor's office and August was depleted. I was physically and emotionally exhausted, but the day, for me, was far from over. I had a commitment to attend the end-of-the-year celebration dinner for the union of SJUSD staff who had endorsed my candidacy for school board. I wanted to thank the group for this important endorsement, but after the grueling day I'd had, I really just wanted to spend the evening with August.

My heart hurt when I dropped August off. I had to remind myself that he would be fine for the few hours I was gone. I drove to the event feeling torn but relieved that the venue was located just a few minutes away from my house.

The dinner was in the cafeteria at one of our local high schools and was packed with staff from the many schools of our district. The room buzzed with the noise of hundreds of people talking and enjoying good food. It wasn't just a celebratory dinner, but a program with speakers which included an introduction of the two candidates endorsed by this union— and I was one of them. This meant that I would have a chance to speak to the biggest audience I had yet to address. Speaking to a room of hundreds of people can be daunting but speaking to such a large group while their attention is on dinner and talking with one another is even more daunting. And, to make matters even more challenging, I was still feeling distracted, wondering how August was doing at home. I realized that the best way for me to get through the moment was to acknowledge how I was feeling and breathe through it.

I had come to the dinner with a speech prepared. But as the first candidate gave her introduction, I decided that I would switch things up. I wanted to share details of my day and all that it had entailed. When it was my turn, the room was still buzzing with noise of many people trying to talk quietly.

I introduced myself, and then I started to tell the story of my son's broken finger. I talked about how I got the call from the school and even though I was worried, I knew August would be okay. I knew he was with the office staff and that they would take good care of him. I talked about how, as a parent, I knew very well how instrumental staff are to schools.

As I continued to talk, the room grew more and more quiet. People had stopped talking to listen to what I had to say. This was a big moment for me in my campaign. I realized that I had the ability to capture an audience. But I also realized that there would be more parent-campaign conflicts ahead, and that my family and I would get through each of those moments as we had on that particular day.

THE ELECTION

Even now, years after the election, I still find it hard to write about losing the election. Campaigning was like sprinting a marathon. Election day was the finish line and the time to find out if my run had provided sufficient momentum and strength to finish with a win.

Getting through election day and waiting for the vote count was the most grueling part of the experience. I came into Tuesday, November 6, with great anticipation, hoping for the best and knowing it was now in the hands of the voters.

November is the busiest time of the year for my department

at work and we are all-hands-on-deck from September to December as my department coordinates our agency's annual conference every December serving over 3,500 attendees. Taking the day off was not an option. I have no memory of the projects I did that day, who I interacted with, or what I ate for lunch. I do know that I deliberately wore a red dress (to channel my inner strength!) and took time to blow out my usually curly hair for a sleeker look. My goal was to survive the day and not let the ball of anxiety sitting in my gut distract me.

I knew election day would be emotionally challenging, so I organized an election watch party with friends, supporters, volunteers, and other allies at a local restaurant where we could gather together. The finish line was in sight, and I wanted to be at the finish line with friends, no matter the outcome.

It was a fun evening with good company and cheer, and even though the tone was supportive and celebratory there was an undercurrent of anticipation as we all waited for the first set of results. The restaurant television was on and around eight p.m. the first results of my race scrolled across the screen to great cheer from our group. The first set of results—the incumbent in first, Myel Jenkins in second, and another candidate trailing in third by a few votes. It was a good sign but not a secure sign, and I left the party even more nervous than I had been when I arrived, knowing that I could readily switch from second place to third, because only a small number of votes provided a cushion between the two

Truth be told, it all became real in the middle of the night when my husband crept out of bed at two in the morning to check updated results. I was conflicted. I really wanted one night of rest without knowing either way, but he was up and checking. He was silent, and that's when I knew, and my heart sank to the depths of my chest. The race was called in late November after weeks of counting votes. The final results— third place for a race with two open seats. I had secured 24 percent of the vote with 40,593 votes and it was not enough to make it a win. It was, and sometimes still is, devastating.

The next day, I got up, got ready for work, and put one foot in front of the other. Moving forward after just losing the race was even more difficult than getting through the anxiety of election day. I wanted to hunker down and cocoon after my loss, but I had to be present, move forward at work, and be present at home for my family who had sacrificed so much during the campaign. Those were hard days; I was deeply disappointed and wrestled with feelings of letting my donors, supporters, and volunteers down. I learned through my loss how deep my community support was. The loss wasn't just mine, but those who were invested in my race shared the pain with me.

ELECTION DETOX

It was important to me to run my campaign in a way that felt authentic. When I lost, I realized that how I approached the results of the election was just as important as how I ran the campaign. With that in mind, I made the decision to be grateful for the experience and for the support I received. That decision helped to mitigate some of the sting of the loss.

After the election, I learned more about the reach of my campaign. One day I went to our neighborhood grocery store to pick up my dry cleaning. I was surprised when the store clerk told me how disappointed he was by the election results. He shared that he and his whole family had voted for me. Then, there was the time I took the boys to the local laser tag place for August's birthday. The clerk who rang up our tickets was a high school student volunteer who had called voters on my behalf in the days before the election. Those are just two stories, but these were weekly occurrences months after the election.

I was so busy campaigning from November 2017 to November 2018 that I never had the time or energy to picture what life would be like after the election. So, when my chaotic campaign schedule suddenly became nonexistent on November 7, it was a shock to my system. I welcomed the new calm, as did my family, but we were all so used to constantly being in motion that it took some time to adjust. August and I made sure to whip up a batch of our traditional cookies that first post-election Saturday. Somehow, too, I had pre-scheduled three massage appointments in the five days following the election. I had to laugh, but I kept all three massage appointments.

In the months after the election, I focused my attention on my family and made time for friends. But I also brought together my solid group of supporters, who had campaigned by my side, for an evening of dinner and discussion. We gathered together in my living room and reminisced about the highs of the campaigns and shared our disappointments about the loss. This brought me closure on the sting of the loss and highlighted the lessons learned, possible strategies for next time, and a recognition of the many successes of my campaign.

RISING FROM THE ASHES

Before deciding to run for office, I had had a long list of fears about the electoral process. I feared that I wouldn't be able to successfully fundraise, that I wouldn't be able to keep up with the pace of campaigning, parenting, and working full time, that campaigning would take a heavy toll on my family. I feared being vulnerable. And my biggest fear of all was losing—not only losing but losing in public. My fears were realistic, but I did not allow them to limit me and my possibilities.

Campaigning was a journey, and in that journey, I made many discoveries about myself. I was surprised to discover that I am a successful fundraiser, and that I had a message that many believed in and were ready to invest in. My motivation to run was fueled by my frustration with the opportunity gaps of our students of color, but particularly for our African American students. I discovered that our community of teachers, staff, parents, and allies are as committed to academic success for all students.

I discovered that I could keep up with the campaign pace because I believed in what I was doing and was committed. While campaigning was hard on my family, each of them was also invested in my race and able to provide support in their own individual ways. I discovered that my marriage of twenty-two years was stronger than I could even imagine. My husband was my greatest cheerleader, and his support at home made it possible for me to run focused and run strong. I learned that campaigning could be a family endeavor; we knocked on doors as a family and talked to voters about why I was the right candidate for school board. I discovered that Dominic could practice driving in preparation for his driving test by driving me to supporters' houses and dropping off lawn signs.

I discovered that my presence in itself as a Black bi-racial working mom running was a success. By entering the race, I was giving permission to all those who look like me to run for office and that it is our right to influence the policies that impact our children and families.

I discovered that being vulnerable is a part of what makes me both authentic and strong. And I discovered that losing is nothing to be afraid of. Losing does not take away from my strength, my commitment, or my accomplishments.

My richest discovery, however, was learning that I did not have to campaign alone. I had a tremendous amount of support from a robust group of friends and allies, a team that believed in me and in my vision for our school district.

The longer I campaigned, the more the group expanded beyond my circle to include parents, teachers, and students in our school district community. These supporters generously donated, hosted house parties to introduce me to their friends and neighbors as a candidate, and volunteered to knock on doors and talk to voters on weekends. To have the support of parents, teachers, and students was one of the most rewarding aspects of campaigning.

The campaign ended with the November election and the dust has settled. I decided to use the months after the election to slow down yet stay involved in the school community. I have mastered the stay-involved part and need to work more on the slow-down part! In the months following the election, I was asked to join a school district appointed committee, the Curriculum and Standards Committee—an opportunity to continue my efforts toward academic achievement for all students. I also joined the board of directors of our local foundation which funds support and services to our schools most in need—a cause that aligns with my passions. I have stayed engaged in local political efforts as an officer with the Women Democratic club of our county and the Black Women of Political Action Sacramento chapter. Both clubs examine and address women's issues in our communities.

For now, I don't have a plan to run again, but I have not ruled out the possibility of a future campaign. While I am enriched from the experience of running, I am taking the time to reconnect with myself, my family, and my community in other ways.

I can say that when I reflect on the experience as a whole, I am in awe. It was a wild ride that I am glad I took. I did not win, but I feel invincible knowing that I took the leap and I survived. I walked away from the election with no regrets. I'm not sure where my journey will take me next and that is okay because I am comfortable with being patient and knowing that I am not at the end. The lessons I learned from campaigning will propel me forward with confidence and strength This experience has reinforced my belief that it is critical to be a part of the spaces in which policies are developed which impact kids, kids of color, and opportunities for achievement.

LESSONS FROM THE LOSS

FINANCES

Myel Jenkins

I knew that I wanted to run, but I didn't know where to start. So, I started by reviewing the California Fair Political Practices Commission (FPPC) website repeatedly and carefully. It was then that I decided my first step would be to hire a campaign treasurer.

I gathered recommendations from my politically savvy friends and connected with one recommended firm. It was December 2017 and I had taken my first step by contracting with a treasurer. I was now committed to a monthly fee—no matter how my fundraising was progressing—but the cost of employing a team of professionals was well worth the peace of mind I gained.

Having a treasurer meant liberating me from the administrative role of opening an election committee and a campaign bank account. And I found that it was worth the monthly fees to have a team tracking incoming donations, outgoing expenses, executing payment of campaign bills and, most importantly, filing the state required election reports.

That investment paid off. It meant that I could devote my campaign time to fundraising and voter outreach rather than focusing on the administrative side of finances—making bank deposits, cutting checks, and completing campaign reports. As a full-time working parent juggling running a grassroots campaign, I was always operating within limited time, and I had to use every moment efficiently.

Once I managed the administrative portion of finances, it

was then time for me to address the emotional aspect. I knew that running a campaign meant that I would be incurring expenses and that these expenses would be beyond my family budget. There was no safety net if my campaign spending exceeded my fundraising, and that was a paralyzing thought. The fear of incurring campaign debt motivated me to make two commitments: 1) to only incur expenses based on the amount of funds available in my campaign account and 2) to limit the amount of family funds that went into the campaign.

Those commitments kept me on track. I had a responsibility to myself to make informed decisions on what to purchase, how much, and when. I worked with the treasurer to receive tracking reports several times a month. With this information, I always knew how much was available and used that information when making decisions, such as, how many newspaper ads to purchase and how many walk pieces (flyers) to order. It was important to me that I be in control of my campaign, even in those areas that were overwhelming, like finances.

These commitments were my motivation to fundraise well. I was determined to bring in enough donations that would allow me to spend on activities that would raise my visibility with the voters.

I started off overwhelmed by the financial aspects of campaigning. The process of working with a treasurer made it less overwhelming. By the time the election came in November, I had gained an enormous amount of experience and was pleased that, when I closed my campaign a month later, I closed with all expenses paid and no debt.

FUNDRAISING

Tara Sreekrishnan

We ran a proud "clean-money" campaign. Altogether, the support we received largely came from community members—often in small, but still meaningful, donations. We raised about

$40,000 by the end of our campaign, 70 percent of which were from donors who gave $50 or less. On principle, we didn't accept corporate money, corporate PAC money, or donations from moneyed interests seeking influence at City Hall. To this end, we also publicly denounced and rejected all independent expenditures from corporate PACs made on our behalf or against other candidates through a public pledge posted on our campaign website. As government becomes increasingly entangled with corporations influencing public discourse and elections, especially through the Supreme Court's Citizens United ruling in 2010, making and fulfilling this pledge was my attempt to increase transparency and trust between the public and their elected representation.

Myel Jenkins

I went into the campaign knowing that effective fundraising was critical to my ability to reach the thousands of voters in our seventy-two-square-mile district. Effective fundraising would give me the ability to purchase walk pieces, digital and newspaper ads, as well as postcards and stamps.

The Emerge California training program gave me the tools to feel more comfortable with fundraising. During training, we practiced the "ask." As a candidate, I was asking my network to invest in me, in my ideas and my vision for the San Juan School District.

I practiced my ask in my first month of fundraising and, in January 2018, I approached my mentors with the ask. Every mentor gave; their donations totaling over $2000. This led to my first experience with the purchasing power that comes with donations. I contracted with a web designer to have my campaign website ready for my announcement in February 2018.

Once I announced, I expanded my fundraising efforts and nervously began making fundraising calls. I squeezed them in during my long commute to and from work and on my lunch hours. The calls worked but were not an overwhelming success.

I have a feeling I would have been more successful if I had invested more time and if I had felt more comfortable with this fundraising technique.

Hosting fundraisers and neighborhood house parties was another successful fundraising strategy. These events could bring in more donations at one time, which was always helpful! We hosted three fundraisers which were spaced two months apart, each one hosted by a different friend. They were successful because of the diligent and consistent outreach of the hosts, as well as myself, to ensure each one was strongly attended. The first fundraiser was the most successful, with over $4,000 raised. The others were also successful in bringing in much appreciated donations.

In addition, there were also eleven different house parties hosted by different friends and supporters from February to October. The house parties, at times, also brought in donations; one in June, was a smaller party than some others but still lovely. Most of the people in attendance donated—including someone who generously donated $500.

The events worked, in part, because of the enormous generosity of the hosts. The hosts provided all food and drink and other party expenses as in-kind donations to my campaign. Their generosity allowed me to focus my campaign costs to other expenses and not have to spend money to raise funds.

What I didn't consider in my campaign was the influx of donations that would come in the final weeks. Leading up to the November 2018 election, I unexpectedly received several thousand dollars in donations. I had a practice of not making big purchases if there was not enough promised or actual funds to cover the costs. This practice kept me from incurring debt, but when the unexpected funds flowed in, I had to move quickly and use the limited days before the race to purchase services, such as more newspaper ads to reach voters. This influx gave me more buying power, but I had to be ready to use it.

The range on where my donations came from echoed the range of my support. Donations came from my mentors, friends near and far, San Juan parents and teachers, neighbors, old and current colleagues, and my family. By September, I surpassed my initial goal of $25,000 and by the end of the campaign I had raised over $30,000. I didn't win the election, but successfully fundraising beyond my goal was a win for me.

CAMPAIGN STAFF AND HIRING

by Jackie Smith

Building a campaign team is the hardest thing to do apart from raising money. You have to find the right staff, and you have to know when to hire them.

As I started my journey to run, many friends came forward to help me; some who are still helping me today in my next run for Assembly. They work as volunteers because we all have the same vision: to get "us" at the Capitol and unseat the incumbent.

When I had raised a bit of money, I hired a part-time assistant to help me with my scheduling, house parties, and volunteer coordination. She became my sidekick and, as the Primary approached, I hired her full time, even putting her to work in the field as we were short staffed. (You'll find that you will need to move people around as the campaign changes.)

A campaign is like a business and it's your job to hire the right people. But also know, just as one needs to protect their business, you must let go of employees when necessary. That was one of the hardest realizations I had to muster.

Many people told me I needed a campaign manager. So, I hired one and, within one month, I had to let him go as it wasn't working out. As a former project manager, I felt I could handle most of the comings/goings while empowering others through team meetings once a week.

A finance/events coordinator is critical to help you with fundraising activities. It is well worth your peace of mind to have them in your corner to help keep things running while you're out in the field.

At the end of the campaign, I had to reorganize the group and push resources toward our field operations. I hired a field director for the last six months of the campaign to help rally the volunteers.

In my campaign, I had hired five people to work for me and no one made less than $15 an hour. I had paid high school interns who worked diligently and were glad to be on the staff. But I had my "super volunteer" friends who came to the rescue to fill in any holes: research, postcards, signage, and phone banks, for example.

During the last four weeks of my campaign, my super volunteer friend came and stayed at my house. She became our campaign manager for the last two months of the campaign. Trust me, at this point of the campaign, you will become overwhelmed with house parties, meetings, and places you have to be, so it is critical to have someone you trust to run operations at the office. I was blessed to have her on my team.

FRIENEMIES

Tara Sreekrishnan

When you're a candidate, everyone says they "support" you. Some of the best guidance I received over the course of my campaign was that someone doesn't really "support" you unless they've proven it to you by 1) publicly endorsing you, 2) donating to your campaign, or 3) knocking on doors for you. Running for office is a process like no other that allows you to gain an understanding of who in your life really supports you. This can definitely be shocking and saddening at times.

ENDORSEMENTS

Myel Jenkins

Going into a campaign for the first time, finances and fundraising seemed overwhelming to me. Learning the endorsement process was no less so. Fundraising and endorsements are linked in some ways. There are times where an endorsement will lead to donations. But they are more linked than just that— when you fundraise, when you ask for an endorsement, you are asking people to invest in you as a candidate, in your ideas, and in your vision. The hope is that people will say, "Yes, I will support your campaign." And there are times that they will say, "No, you are not the candidate that I will support." That is what made endorsements such a rich and mixed experience for me.

One of my early informational interviews was with a local elected official. He was someone who was easy to approach because our professional lives had crossed paths multiple times over the years. We met over coffee and he gave advice on how to approach endorsements: "There are three kinds—the ones that bring donations, the ones that bring campaign volunteers, and the ones that will bring you more voters."

That was advice I held onto, especially when I began to understand that Sacramento is a region rich with endorsement opportunities. Sacramento is California's capitol, and the region is full of state and local elected officials, unions and Democratic clubs.

Gaining endorsements meant many coffee meetings, attendance at different Democratic clubs, responding to endorsement questionnaires, participating in endorsement interviews, and sometimes even brief participations at meetings. Endorsements were both an investment of time and effort.

I participated in the endorsement process for over fifteen organizations from February to October 2018. This included local Democratic clubs, as well as unions of the San Juan School District and Sacramento region unions. There were more opportunities available beyond the ones I participated in, but I just did not have the capacity to make those happen.

There were times when multiple clubs had deadlines in the same weeks, and I would have to work with my consultant to prioritize which questionnaires to complete. The organizations that were most aligned with my values and who could contribute to my campaign became the ones that I prioritized. Of those fifteen organizational endorsement processes that I participated in, I received ten endorsements. It was an honor to receive each of those donations, and it was a special honor to be endorsed by all four of the San Juan School District unions and associations that got involved in the race. The support from these endorsements was tremendous and ranged from promoting my campaign, contributing volunteers for precinct walking as well as voter calls, to lawn sign distribution, to funding and sending voter campaign mailers, and donating to the campaign.

This is not to say that I wasn't disappointed to not gain the other endorsements. In particular, there were a few endorsement situations which involved heated discussions about each of us as candidates. Discussions would focus on why some of us in our school board race would, and why some would not, be the best candidate for an endorsement. These times were the most challenging for me—it's rare that I have been in a room where people talked about my challenges and strengths.

I admit, hearing those discussions stung; not getting the endorsements stung too. But I was not going to see those as setbacks but as part of the rigors of campaigning. How I handled a loss reflected my character and strength just as much as how I handled a success.

Field Campaign and "Get-Out-The-Vote"

Jackie Smith

Having a great field campaign is the best way to win. We had limited resources and decided to focus on fifty-three precincts that weren't being touched by the Congressional campaigns in Congressional District 4.

Using the campaign database, PDI, and partnering with other candidates, we, with our small group of volunteers, worked every weekend to canvas. PDI lists become critical in targeting specific voters.

Your car, in the beginning, will become your campaign office on wheels. I drive an older 2012 Lincoln Hybrid which was stocked with campaign swag, signs, T-shirts, and clipboards. My fuel-efficient car really took a beating. For sustenance, I learned to keep granola bars and a case of water in the trunk. Being a vegetarian and non-drinker, I had to plan ahead before a function as seemingly every one was a wine and cheese soiree, neither of which I normally partake, so I was always chasing nourishment along the trail in between functions.

The last month up to the last days before election day, we conducted text banking and robocalls targeting specific groups in the community.

PR and Marketing

Tara Sreekrishnan

Our campaign was able to afford only two mailers over the course of the campaign. These reached the doors of all likely voters in the city—those who voted in at least three out of the five elections. Given the recent election of Trump, in hindsight, it would have been more effective to send mail to every voter in the city as many "unlikely" voters were energized to vote from the undemocratic policies barreling through the White House from the Trump administration.

In contrast, it seemed like every day we were bombarded by mailers paid for by developers for or against the other candidates. The attack mailers backfired; they were much more effective in garnering sympathy and support for the candidates they opposed, eventually helping lead them to victory.

Top List of Takeaways

Ways Friends Can Support Their Candidate

1. Host a house party for your candidate and invite everyone you know

2. Step in for the candidate and pick up, or drop off, their kids when they're double-booked

3. Write campaign postcards on why you're voting for your candidate

4. Go to a candidate forum, smile from the audience, and clap loudly

5. Wear the candidate's campaign stickers EVERYWHERE

6. Go with the candidate to a campaign event as their "Plus 1"

7. Pick up a boatload of campaign lawn signs and deliver them to your family and neighbors

8. Text a pick-me up "you got this!" or "I'm glad you're running" text periodically

9. If they have any free time, take them to do something normal and non-campaign related, like to brunch, drinks, or a movie

10. Aggressively pass around donation envelopes and volunteer sign-up sheets on behalf of the candidate

11. Introduce your candidate to your network and influencers in the community that they may not know

12. Drop off comfort food

13. Be honest with any feedback for the candidate, even if you disagree with the candidate's professional consultants

14. The week before the election, send a personal card or gift

15. Ask how you can help

Ways to Stay Fueled, Inspired and Sane on the Campaign Trail

1. Build a playlist of fight songs and listen to it loudly in between events

2. Have a spare pair of comfortable shoes in your car or bag at all times

3. Carry some kind of snack (granola bars, almonds, etc.) in your bag at all times

4. Get some rest when you can; naps are your friend

5. If you have a partner, be sure they are 100 percent on board with you running

6. Ask friends for help when you need it; for instance, ask them to drive you if you have a hectic event schedule

7. Pick something that is all about you and makes you feel grounded: a regular yoga routine, reading a book, a round of golf, regular morning walks, going to Church, or dropping your kids off in the mornings; build that one-thing into your weekly routine, even if it's only once a week for a few minutes

8. Give yourself campaign office hours and stop answering emails after your office hours end; don't do important work when you're tired

9. Make "crockpots" your friend

10. Surround yourself with staff, volunteers, friends, and family who you trust

11. Don't be afraid to let go of certain family responsibilities and transfer them to others or your partner; let go of any guilt
12. Say "No" when you can; remember "No" is a complete sentence
13. Pick your "ride or die" friends and text/call them when you need a pick me up or inspirational quote
14. Be kind to yourself
15. Remind yourself why you're running

Campaign "Fight" Music

1. "Fight Song" by Rachel Platten
2. "San Francisco Bay Blues" by Eric Clapton
3. "Hero" by Mariah Carey
4. "My Shot" from the Hamilton Soundtrack
5. "Lose Yourself" by Eminem
6. "Superwoman" by Alicia Keyes
7. "Turn, Turn, Turn" by Judy Collins
8. "Taking it to the Streets" by The Doobie Brothers
9. "Sabotage" by the Beastie Boys
10. Cinnamon Girl" by Neil Young
11. "Gravity" by Allison Krause
12. "Over the Rainbow" with Eva Cassidy and Chuck Brown
13. "No Light, No Light" by Florence and the Machine
14. Anything by Beyonce, and especially, "Run the World (Girls), "Formation," and "Freedom"

How Women Can Support Other Women in Politics

1. Identify "Fementors" (female mentors)
2. Speak up when another female candidate is being dismissed; validate other women
3. Don't engage in gossip against female candidates
4. Create and support networks of female candidates or other women in politics; women need to stand up for other women
5. Get out the vote!
6. Write a check
7. Write letters to the editor, post positive social media comments, and endorse other women
8. Get the word out in your network for other female candidates and make introductions
9. Tell women to run for office; tell them at least three times!
10. Encourage other women, of all ages and backgrounds, to proactively engage in the political process

A LETTER TO MY NIECE

By California State Treasurer Fiona Ma

To my niece Kimberly:

You will be eligible to vote in two years. I know registering to vote is probably not the first thing you are looking forward to doing on your eighteenth birthday. Frankly, it was not on my to-do list either at eighteen, but I hope it will be on yours.

I know you really liked President Obama. He and Michelle were amazing role models, and we watched his two daughters Malia and Sasha grow up—in the White House. They knew, as a minority family serving in the most prestigious position in the world, that all eyes were watching them every day and some people were hoping that they would mess up, but they did not. The Obama family served with distinction for their entire eight years.

When Hillary Rodman Clinton (HRC) decided to run again in 2016, I signed up early and I knew you followed the election and rooted for HRC. We felt it was finally OUR time for a woman to be president especially since more than half of our population are women. Up until 2016, I didn't think I would ever see a woman president, but Hillary was the most qualified presidential candidate we've ever had in modern times, so I was hopeful. Although she did not win, she sparked a movement. Women woke up and started posting on Facebook to join the Women's March. "If not us, then who?" was the new mantra. If Donald Trump could get elected with no political experience, what were women waiting for?

The year 2017 became the second "Year of the Woman" in the U.S. The first one was in 1992 when we got Dianne Feinstein and Barbara Boxer elected as U.S. senators on the heels of the

Anita Hill testimony. An estimated 200,000 marchers showed up in Washington, DC, on January 21, 2017, and five million people took to the streets worldwide following the Trump election.

In 2017, more and more women showed up at Democratic Club meetings and more women, including your grandma, wanted to join the 2018 Women's March. We saw a record number of women pulling papers to run for office that November, at all levels of government, including the women featured in this book. And although Hillary didn't win, she opened a path to more than five qualified women candidates running for president in 2020.

When asked about what it is like for women in politics, I use the Fred Astaire and Ginger Rogers analogy: Ginger did everything Fred did but backwards and in high heels. And that's what it's like to run for office and that's what it's like every day once we assume an elected position. So, I hope you read this book, Kimberly, and you are inspired to make a difference. I applaud my sisters for sharing their stories and for being our generation's Pathfinders. It's our time, ladies, and it's always the right time to step up! Keep Calm and Run for Office!

Appendix

Resources for Women Running for Office

Candidate Boot Camp
https://candidatebootcamp.com/about/
Candidate Boot Camp is a team of experienced campaign professionals with a goal to democratize democracy by lowering the barriers to running for political office.

Center for American Women and Politics
https://cawp.rutgers.edu/
The Center for American Women and Politics houses the Women's Political Power Map with a link to resources across the nation.

EMERGE America
https://emergeamerica.org/
Emerge America is a national training program that inspires women to run, hone their skills and win.

Emily's List Training Center
https://trainingcenter.emilyslist.org/
Emily's List trains pro-choice Democratic women to run for office.

Her Time
https://www.her-time.com/
Her Time supports women and young people—often the long-shot candidates who have the vision and drive needed to make lasting systemic change—who don't yet have the resources that come with being a proven or established politician.

Ignite
https://www.ignitenational.org/training
Ignite is a movement of young women who are ready and eager to become the next generation of political leaders.

LGBT Victory Institute Candidate and Campaign Training
https://victoryinstitute.org/trainings/candidate-campaign-trainings/
The Victory Institutes intensive four-day Candidate & Campaign Trainings provide comprehensive, non-partisan best practices to present and future LGBTQ candidates, campaign staff and community leaders.

LPAC
https://www.teamlpac.com/
LPAC builds political strength and increases representation for and with LGBTQ women.

National Organization for Women PAC
https://www.nowpac.org/
NWPC-PAC supports pro-choice women candidates from around the country.

National Women's Political Caucus
https://www.nwpc.org/
NWPC is a national, proc-choice, multi-partisan, grassroots membership organization dedicated to identifying, recruiting, training and supporting women candidates for elected and appointed offices.

Off the Sidelines
https://offthesidelines.org/resources/
Through her Off the Sidelines PAC, Senator Kirsten Gillibrand is committed to electing more women to Congress and supporting allies who share progressive values.

Ready to Run
https://cawp.rutgers.edu/education_training/ready_to_run/overview
Ready to Run is a national network of non-partisan campaign training programs committed to electing more women to public office.

Run Women Run
http://www.runwomenrun.org/

Run Women Run is a nonpartisan organization that inspires, recruits, and trains qualified, pro-choice women to seek elected and appointed office.

Teach a Girl to Lead

http://tag.rutgers.edu/

Teach a Girl to Lead is making women's public leadership visible to the next generation.

Vote Mama

https://www.votemama.org/

Vote Mama, led by former congressional candidate Liuba Grechen Shirley, supports Democratic moms with young children running for office up and down the ballot and across the country.

Women's Campaign Fund PAC

http://www.wcfonline.org/about_wcf_pac

Women's Campaign Fund is the first national organization in the country to financially support women candidates. They are dedicated to supporting the advancement of strong, women leaders of all parties and at all levels of government.